天符經

Cheon Bu Gyeong

The principle of a cosmic evolutionary path walked by God

天符經

Cheon Bu Gyeong

The principle of a cosmic
evolutionary path walked by God

Written by Sang-Young Han
Translated by Seong-Uk Park / Kwang-Soo Shin

Jisik Gonggam Publishing Company

Notice

1. This book is based on the namesake original text 「Cheon Bu Gyeong, The principle of a cosmic evolutionary path walked by God」. The original text is composed of 「Cheon Bu Gyeong Deconstructed」, 「Introduction; Human, the border between change and evolution of the cosmos」, 「Five chapters (Chapter 1; The theory of BonSim in the Cheon Bu Gyeong/ Chapter 2; Structural principle and interpretation system/ Chapter 3; Explanations of the original text/ Chapter 4; Clarification on the explanations of the original text-human and God, the Earth, the cosmos and the absolute Mu/ Chapter 5; The principle of the Yeok Gyeong (I Ching in Chinese) and the Do Deok Gyeong (Tao Te Ching in Chinese) explained only by the Cheon Bu Gyeong)」, 「Appendix; Ideology and numbers in the Cheon Bu Gyeong」

2. In 2,333 B.C. 'HongIkInGan (弘益人間)' and 'JaeSeIHwa (在世理化)' became the founding ideology and the ruling philosophy of the ancient Korean kingdom Gojoseon (古朝鮮, 2,333-108 B.C) and remain so to the present time in Korea. 'HongIkInGan (弘益人間)' and 'JaeSeIHwa (在世理化)', which are Korea's indigenous human philosophy and community spirit, are the world view completed by the cosmic principle of the Cheon Bu Gyeong.

   - **HongIkInGan** (弘益人間): HongIkInGan (弘益人間) has a meaning not only as a role, 'benefiting humans far and wide', but also as a being, 'people who benefit humans far and wide'. In the Cheon Bu Gyeong HongIkInGan (弘益人間) is the existential symbol of human with BonSim, and the role of HongIkInGan (弘益人間) is to make other people have BonSim.

   - **JaeSeIHwa** (在世理化), **IHwaSeGye** (理化世界): JaeSeIHwa (在世理化) is to make the world correspond to the cosmic principle by letting human evolve into HongIkInGan (弘益人間), and the world filled with 'HongIkInGan (弘益人間) who benefits humans far and wide' through this is IHwaSeGye (理化世界).

Contents

Chapter 1
Cheon Bu Gyeong (天符經) Deconstructed ········· 9

Human trapped inside the world ········· 11
The weapon of the world, survival ········· 14
Finishing the vacation of human ········· 17
Value of the Cheon Bu Gyeong ········· 19
Origin and controversy of the Cheon Bu Gyeong ········· 22
The principle of the Cheon Bu Gyeong ········· 27
The obligation as a people of the descendants from the sky ········· 33
The usage of the Cheon Bu Gyeong ········· 38

Chapter 2
The structural principle of the Cheon Bu Gyeong (天符經) ···· 43

Chapter 3
Explanations of the original text of the Cheon Bu Gyeong ·· 49

IlSiMuSill (一始無始一), SeokSamGeuk (析三極), MuJinBon (無盡本) ········ 52
  One begins and it begins from Mu / Divided into SamGeuk (Three Geuks) / An inexhaustible Bon (the Root).

CheonIlIl, JiIlI, InIlSam (天一一, 地一二, 人一三) ········· 73
　Cheon is Il (One), Ji is I (Two) and In is Sam (Three) in the first operation.

IlJeokSipGeo (一積十鉅), MuGweHwaSam (無櫃化三) ········· 80
　Accumulated One by One expands up to Sip (Ten) / When Gwe is extinct, it becomes Sam (Three).

CheonIlSam, JilSam, InIlSam (天二三, 地二三, 人二三) ········· 91
　Cheon is Sam (Three), Ji is Sam (Three) and In is Sam (Three) as well in the second operation.

DaeSamHapYuk (大三合六), SaengChilPalGu (生七八九) ········· 98
　Sam (Three) is expanded and combined into Yuk (Six) / To be born as Chil (Seven), Pal (Eight) and Gu (Nine).

UnSam (運三), SaSeong (四成), HwanOChil (環五七) ········· 111
　The principle of operation is Sam (Three) / The principle of completion is Sa (Four) / The principle of circulation is O (Five) and Chil (Seven).

IlMyoYeon (一妙衍), ManWangManRae (萬往萬來), YongByeonBuDongBon(用變不動本) ········· 127
　The flow of Il (One) is mysterious / Even though it comes and goes ten thousand times / Usage changes but Bon does not move.

BonSim (本心), BonTaeYangAngMyeong (本太陽昂明), InJungCheonJiIl (人中天地一) ·········· 140

Bon is Sim (the Mind) / When looking up to Bon, the brightness of the Sun / Cheon and Ji becomes Il (One) inside In (Human).

IlJongMuJongIl (一終無終一) ·········· 156

Il (One) finishes and it finishes as Mu.

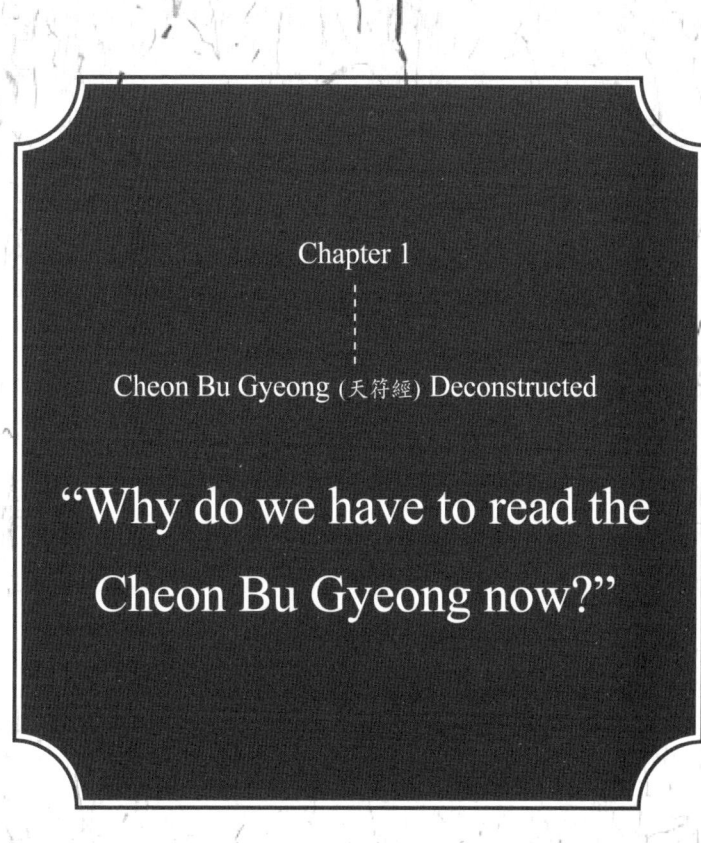

[Cheon Bu Gyeong (天符經) Deconstructed]
Why do we have to read the Cheon Bu Gyeong now?

Human trapped inside the world

The world is a man-made space between the sky and the earth made by human, for human, and only shared among humans. While the human world was being created, human consciousness has been separated from God and the cosmos. It is because only choices needed for the worldly life were repeated. And through this process, civilization and religion became the two pillars of the world. As the intelligence of civilization teaches the life as an earthly being, humans became trapped in the earthly changes instead of undergoing a cosmic evolution. Furthermore, as religion replaces God, the existential evolutionary link connected to God has also been broken. The purpose and process of the cosmos creating the Earth and selecting human as the main agents of the operation has been forgotten.

The mentality connecting the cosmos and human has also been deteriorated through this process. It shrank to an earthly matter connecting human and the Earth, and ultimately became permanent as a worldly matter connecting humans. Humans unraveled their link with the cosmos by themselves and came to regard the world, just an island on the Earth, as the entirety of human.

The cosmos created the Earth in a state of Mu with the Mu of the cosmos. And it made the Earth operate to create human who will play a role in accordance with the purpose of the cosmos. The purpose is a cosmic evolution into God mentioned in the Cheon Bu Gyeong. It helps humans return to the right path out of being trapped inside the world. The Cheon Bu Gyeong explains only by eighty-one letters about the emergence and purpose of the cosmos, the Earth, and human, as well as the whole evolutionary path that human must walk. The reason why the Cheon Bu Gyeong is composed of such a short scripture is to preserve the clear principle. This means that there is a clear purpose bestowed upon the existence of human. And it is Buddha, Jesus and Lao Tzu that have shown the way according with the purpose. This is a cosmic evolutionary path, and at the end of this path human becomes God. It is all attributed to the people who have become Gods that humans have not gone extinct even though they have forgotten the path and been trapped inside the world.

Humans have worshiped them as Gods of the Earth. And they just live following these Gods used by the world rather than pursuing the cosmic principle to become Gods like they did. It is because they lost their original divinity, the Mind (心), while trapped in the world. So most humans have only a place for the Mind. Human is the only being on the Earth who evolved suitable for the path in accordance with the cosmos. By a clear purpose of the cosmos, the Earth had been created in the cosmos and then human was created on the Earth. The people who kept the purpose, the purity of evolution, became Buddha, Jesus, and Lao Tzu. The Cheon Bu Gyeong clearly demonstrates the principle of walking the evolutionary path. From the moment human was selected to be the only being suitable for the purpose of the cosmos, the existential role of human is not a matter of choice. So 'I in the world' is an opportunity for life afforded to 'I as a human evolving into God'. Humans trapped inside the world should escape the borders on their own and restore their existences.

The weapon of the world, survival

The world of human is mainly divided into 'the world based on civilization' and 'the world based on mentality'. Humans cannot realize the existential life because they live with believing that the two types of the world taught by civilization and mentality are the whole. These two extremes of the world have several things in common. Firstly, both of them claim that they are for humans. Secondly, they dominate humans by teaching that they are the only options for humans. Thirdly, they regard humans as poor beings in need of care since humans cannot stand alone. Lastly these two worlds are limited to the very small world inside the Earth and created by neither God nor the cosmos but by human. For a long time, humans have established standards by the repetition of self-restriction through voluntary subordination, and shared the faith that the world is the whole. It was possible because the world succeeded in planting fear of survival inside human.

Survival has been taught to human by the world represented by civilization and religion. Survival is a tool that drags death into the area of human consciousness. Originally survival and death were only natural processes of human life. But they became special as they were given significance by civilization and religion. Civilization caused human beings to compete over the value of survival and religion decorated survival with patterns of transience and obedience. Through these processes, the extreme standards of human life became permanent and the mixture of desire for survival and fear of death made humans become obsessive about life. It made people forget the fact that originally survival is not a purpose but just a repeated opportunity. Mistaking the means for the end like this, human consciousness became limited to the world and lost its freedom. Therefore, as long as humans depend on these two worlds they will never reach the level of consciousness where they can walk freely the path of human life.

Humans have developed these properties and principles of civilization and religion for thousands of years. The intellectuals and religious men inside the world are people located at the peak of this consciousness. Therefore, it is difficult for them to intactly pass on the scriptures and teachings of Buddha, Jesus and Lao Tzu who became Gods through walking the path of human life. With the level of human consciousness accustomed to the order established by the world, humans cannot understand the essence of them who have different starting point and purpose of consciousness. This means that people cannot understand the reason why human became the central existence of the Earth and the principle how the Earth emerged in the cosmos. And it is proven by the earthly reality that people who have become Gods do not emerge anymore. The limits of these two worlds which are the borders of humans became apparent and the cosmos gave humans a vacation so that they can correct them by themselves. Humans do not have meaning just because they are humans. Humans have earthly meaning because they were selected as a being in accordance with the purpose of the cosmos, and they should realize that they could have cosmic value of existence only when they continue to accord with the purpose of the cosmos. Thus, the path of human life cannot be found in the world. Human must find the path in the existential meaning of human. The classics and scriptures show the answers to the path. Through this, human must focus on the existential value and the evolutionary meaning of human.

Finishing the vacation of human

The size of the world has a huge impact on the stability of the Earth which is a separated and fixed time and space. As the world becomes larger, it becomes more difficult for the Earth to continue the original existential purpose, and human consciousness becomes prevented from extending into the Earth or the cosmos. And it deteriorates the relationships between humans as well as between human and the Earth from cooperation and coexistence to competition and domination. The problem is that if civilization and religion reach their limits, they will not be able to present attractive alternatives to human any longer. Now is the breaking point when the existential value of human has disappeared and the number has reached the maximum amount. Human has no choice but to return to the being that used to be able to evolve. Therefore, people who realized that they could not receive answers from the world have begun to search the way of consciousness connected to the cosmos. The proof of this move is that questions about God, the cosmos, spirituality, and consciousness revolution are raised mainly in the west. However, they have no alternatives among themselves that can answer the questions so the mainstream is made up with people who believe in such thing as alien civilizations. Nevertheless, it is clear that human has begun to try to communicate directly with the cosmos escaping from the stereotype and dominance of civilization and encounter Gods per se regardless of religions.

Now the vacation of human thanks to the people who have become Gods is over. Humans must walk the original path where they kept the opportunity and existential value, and pursue the cosmic divinity beyond the convenience of civilization and science. Information about this issue is flooding the world now more than ever. Civilization, religion and an inertial life adjusting to changes can no longer provide alternatives. By pursuing 'the reason why they have survived on the Earth' rather than 'surviving on the Earth', human must correct the root of consciousness and the opportunity of survival according with the original purpose of human emergence. The only alternative for this is not to change within the limited time and space, but to live with a cosmic evolutionary consciousness beyond the border of time and space. The Cheon Bu Gyeong teaches that it is the evolution from human, a being based on the earthly Mu into God, a being based on the cosmic Mu. The original existential role of human can be found in the Cheon Bu Gyeong. The reason why the Cheon Bu Gyeong which had been passed down as esoteric knowledge was revealed around 100 years ago can be also understood in this big trend.

Value of the Cheon Bu Gyeong

Originally human had never kept borders between nature and the world, God and human, or the cosmos and the Earth. Everything was connected to the single Bon (本, the Root) and path. In the myths of the world, the traces remain intact. It was possible for human to reach the end of the evolutionary path and finish. The Cheon Bu Gyeong is a scripture in regard to the existence and purpose of the cosmos, the Earth and human not in a myth form but as a complete principle. It shows the principle by which the cosmos and the Earth, God and human are connected through a single time and space without borders. It is possible because all of them are created with one single Mu. In other words, the single Mu has been established as a being, time and space corresponding to the purpose, which means the cosmos, the Earth and human. Therefore, the Cheon Bu Gyeong can teach that human evolves from a being of all creation into an earthly being and then evolves again into a cosmic being.

Thus, it is only the Cheon Bu Gyeong that can provide a coherent principle behind the creation of human and the Earth as well as in the existence and purpose of human. Buddha, Jesus and Lao Tzu followed this principle and became Gods, Mu of the cosmos. However, mentality and civilization, a mixture of their teachings and human desires have strayed from the path. In order to return to the path, a complete map and justification are needed. This is the basic value of the Cheon Bu Gyeong. What the Cheon Bu Gyeong communicates is the original way of life that people had lived before they had fear and the original brightness that they had pursued before they were trapped inside the world. The Cheon Bu Gyeong makes human realize that for human there is a way of life in accordance with the sky, that is to say the cosmic purpose. It is the true path of human life, which has nothing to do with 'living well', 'living long' or 'waiting for death' that the world teaches. It is not to live for survival but to use their lives as opportunities.

Humans must be able to use their lives fully for themselves. For this, humans need a tool to help them cross the border of consciousness which was trapped immediately after the birth. The Cheon Bu Gyeong is the appropriate scripture for this role. It is to change the root, the starting point of consciousness, by facing Gods and the cosmos without going through the world and religion. Through this it shows that humans exist for a different purpose from what is taught by religion, civilization, culture or knowledge. It is to find grounds for the conversion of consciousness to regain the essence of human existence. If humans accept the reason why they are the main character of an earthly evolution, they cannot lose the opportunities given to the current lives. For humans, this process is not to progress but to correct regression. It is proved by the reality that humans cannot go beyond the past experiences of people who have become Gods. Returning to the original level of consciousness with which humans could evolve into Gods is to restore the value of human existence. The Cheon Bu Gyeong becomes the root of the converted consciousness, and its stem and fruit are scriptures such as the Yeok Gyeong (易經, I Ching in Chinese) and the Do Deok Gyeong (道德經, Tao Te Ching in Chinese). In this way, the Cheon Bu Gyeong is the only scripture to prove the root of human existence and value of human in the cosmos.

Origin and controversy of the Cheon Bu Gyeong

The Cheon Bu Gyeong talks about human free from all civilization and religion, and the essence of God symbolized as Mu (無). It is the principle and reason of existence of the cosmos, and is also the evolutionary journey that human walks as a main character. For this reason, the Cheon Bu Gyeong which conveys the principle of the cosmic evolution into God is absolutely necessary for human of the present time. Originally human consciousness was open from the Earth into the cosmos. Therefore, at that time human consciousness followed the Sun and numerous Gods of stars. Humans were not the beings too burdened to even follow Gods on the Earth. The Cheon Bu Gyeong is reviving the broken roots of consciousness to its intact form. To live without knowing the purpose of human emerging on the Earth makes the repetitive process of life and death meaningless. There is a clear purpose in human life, and they have to try to walk the path by themselves.

The Cheon Bu Gyeong is the greatest scripture of the Korean people. It is composed of eighty-one letters and contains the operating principle of the cosmos. According to tradition, the Cheon Bu Gyeong had begun in Hwan (桓) Empire era as Hwan Woong (桓雄) had commanded Shinji Hyeokdeok (神誌赫德) to write in ancient character, Nokdomun (鹿圖文), and it had been passed down in Jeon character (篆書) during Dangun (檀君) era. In the Silla era, Chiwon Choi (崔致遠) translated the passage on the Dangun stone tablet discovered in the Taebaek Mountain into Chinese character, and that is the current version of the Cheon Bu Gyeong. The ascetic Yeonsoo Gye (桂

延壽) discovered the eighty-one letters carved on the stone walls of Myohyang Mountain in 1917 and imparted it to Dangunism (檀君敎, the religion of Dangun worship), thereby the Cheon Bu Gyeong became known to the world. Documents containing the original text or name of the Cheon Bu Gyeong are the Taebaekilsa (太白逸史), Samseonggi (三聖記), Dangunsegi (檀君世記), Dangigosa (檀奇古史), Samgukyusa (三國遺事), Cheoneuljingyeong (天乙眞經), Nongeunyujipbon (農隱遺集本), etc. There are various versions of the Cheon Bu Gyeong such as the Myohyangsan Seokbyeokbon (石壁本), Choigoun Sajeokbon (事蹟本), Taebaekilsabon (太白逸史本) and Nohsajeonbon (盧沙傳本). And Myohyangsan Seokbyeokbon is the accepted version.

The scripture of the Cheon Bu Gyeong varies slightly depending on the version. But the structure remains the same, and there is little semantical difference. There is controversy that the Cheon Bu Gyeong is a fake scripture due to its ambiguous source. It is because the Cheon Bu Gyeong lacks bibliographical evidence and questions about its reliability are raised constantly. The controversy is similar to that over oracle bone script (甲骨文) before it was discovered in the 20th century. Oracle bone script also had been a subject of controversy for the same reason until the 19th century. Similarly, there had been constant controversies surrounding the history and culture of that era. This shows the limit of the way of accepting facts through the basis. Nevertheless, the academic basis such as era, literature, and leading concept of history is still being used as a major tool for confirming facts.

The Cheon Bu Gyeong had been a natural principle in ancient times but changed to esoteric knowledge in the process of being passed down. In addition, the scripture is composed of only eighty-one letters, which makes it short and simple. Hence there was no need to be passed down or educated in a book form. The controversy that the Cheon Bu Gyeong is a fake scripture is caused by lack of understanding on these characteristics. Another reason is that the consciousness lowered by corrupted mentality lost the capability to intuitively accept the truth or facts of the scripture. If people are able to understand the structure and principle of the Cheon Bu Gyeong, they can see that the Cheon Bu Gyeong shares the roots with longstanding traditions such as 'HongIkInGan (弘益人間)' and 'JaeSeIHwa (在世

理化)'. There are not many truths that can be proven by the accumulated beliefs or knowledge of human. When it comes to ancient traditions such as Oracle bone script and the Cheon Bu Gyeong, it is all the more so.

The limit of human consciousness has been narrowed as the human world has downscaled from a cosmic life to an earthly life and finally to a human life. This is because humans follow man-made brightness rather than the original brightness of the cosmos. Fortunately, there are immortal roots in the Cheon Bu Gyeong, 'HongIkInGan (弘益人間)' and 'JaeSeIHwa (在世理化)', which can verify the scriptures. The Cheon Bu Gyeong is a scripture for human. It is the textbook that teaches the reason why humans exist in the cosmos and the path of human life in accordance with it. If the Cheon Bu Gyeong regains its original usage by proving that the ideologies of 'HongIkInGan (弘益人間)' and 'IHwaSeGye (理化世界)' came from it, the controversy that it is a fake scripture will be resolved naturally. It is to authenticate the fact whether it corresponds to the essence of the root of human emergence. And it is the original way of learning. Through this process, humans must find what is right among the knowledge of the world. And by pursuing it, they have to improve their ability to elucidate the original principle. The principle of cosmic evolution in the Cheon Bu Gyeong can be the standard. It is the compass and learning material appropriate for the journey of regaining the original form of human where the Mind naturally faces the brightness.

The principle of the Cheon Bu Gyeong

The Cheon Bu Gyeong is a scripture that teaches the path of human to reach a being of Mu, a state of independent One, by pursuing the principle of the sky. The principle by which the Earth becomes independent in a state of Mu from the cosmos through IlSiMuSill (一始無始一) is applied to human. However, there is a difference between human and the Earth in that the Earth begins as One and becomes independent from the cosmos, but human becomes One through IlJongMuJongIl (一終無終一) and goes back to the cosmos from the Earth. The Cheon Bu Gyeong imparts that the original purpose of human is to go through the principle and process like this. One indicates the being that has its own independent time and space. Generally, the cosmos is One and the Earth is One. However, human is not a complete One like the cosmos or the Earth. In order to become One, human must be in a state of InJungCheonJill (人中天地一) where he has the same size with the Earth. Human in a state of complete One is called God. Only after human becomes God, he can be One that can bear other humans with his own time and space like the cosmos and the Earth. This cosmic evolution in the Cheon Bu Gyeong is possible because separate times and spaces are connected with each other leaning on Mu. The cosmos and the Earth function as the bases. And on them humans evolve from earthly beings into cosmic beings through their own existential evolution.

Existence is having a role in accordance with the principle of the cosmos. Therefore, each One has its own existence. There is no relativity. Relativity explains the changes that occur in the time and space of the Earth. This is the different principle from the existence of Mu which is composed of the visible and the invisible. For this reason, 'Mu Guek (無極, Wuji in Chinese)', 'Tae Geuk (太極, Taiji in Chinese)', 'Eum Yang (陰陽, Yin and Yang in Chinese)', and 'O Haeng (五行, the five elements, Wu xing in Chinese)' must be understood as the principles of changes restricted in the Earth on the cosmic evolutionary path. The Cheon Bu Gyeong clearly states that humans cannot experience cosmic evolution without going beyond relativity and realizing the individual existence. It is also the same reason why the Yeok Gyeong (易經, I Ching in Chinese) and the Do Deok Gyeong (道德經, Tao Te Ching in Chinese) which follows the principle of cosmic evolution explain not by principle or concept of relativity, but by existence and role. This means that there could be no relativity because all the beings are based on the same character, Mu. A time and space can only survive by relying on the bigger time and space which created it. Hence, the Earth can be operated only as the role in accordance with the cosmic purpose. Humans are also operated in accordance with the purpose of the Earth by the same principle. Through this it can be known that the purpose of the cosmos is not time and space, but the beings in the time and space. The Cheon Bu Gyeong clarifies that the cosmos, the Earth, and human, that are linked through Mu do not exist simply to be maintained.

Mu (無, the state before the Big Bang, zero, nothing, extinct)

Mu in the Cheon Bu Gyeong is the existential principle of the cosmos. The Cheon Bu Gyeong contains the content and evolutionary principle as follows; 'One that has begun from Mu' creates 'One that has begun as Mu'. This 'One that has begun as Mu' goes through the process of Un Sam (運三, three operations), and then 'finish' to be 'new One in a state of Mu'. This means that a being that has begun from Mu becomes equal to the Mu. Mu in the Cheon Bu Gyeong is not the Mu of 'presence or absence', but the essence of existence. This is the reason why the Cheon Bu Gyeong begins in a state of Mu and finishes in a state of Mu. 'One that has begun from Mu' means the cosmos from the Absolute Mu, the Earth from the cosmos, and all creation from the Earth. It is human that was selected by the Earth as an appropriate being for evolution among all creation. Everything is Mu in the cosmos. Only characters vary according to the being, time and space. Therefore, the essence of Mu does not change. Only characters as well as time and space of Mu vary according to stop (死) and finish (終). Humans reach the state of InJungCheonJill (人中天地一) which is the same state of Mu as the cosmos creates the Earth by pursuing the brightness of the sun (太陽昂明),

the symbol of Mu that created the Earth. Through the finish, 'One that has begun as Mu' becomes the size of Sip (Ten) which is the same size of the Earth where it had begun. Therefore it is called 'One that has finished as Mu (無終一)'. Mu of IlSiMuSiIl (一始無始一) and Mu of IlJongMuJongIl (一終無終一) are semantically the same, however they symbolize totally different characters changed through evolution. Humans call those who have arrived at MuJongIl (無終一) as Gods.

Bon (本, the Root)

Bon (本, the Root) symbolizes the completed state of One. Humans can be connected to the cosmos and the Earth which are in the completed state, only after they arrives at their BonSim (本心). The Cheon Bu Gyeong sets the Sun as the cosmic Bon that the cosmos planted for the Earth. For this reason the Earth lives following the brightness of the Sun. In this way, the Bon of the Earth is SamGeuk (三極) of SeokSamGeuk (析三極). On the same principle as the cosmos creates the Earth, the Earth creates CheonJiIn (天地人) SamJae (三才) reliant on its Bon, SamGeuk. And the Earth operates SamJae like the cosmos operates the Earth. The fruit of the operation is human, and BonSim is the state of human having Bon.

The Earth holds human on the same principle as the cosmos holds the Earth. Like this the cosmos, the Earth, and human are linked together in a state of Bon. Since then, human lives as a being in accordance with the purpose of the cosmos. The Cheon Bu Gyeong shows that the purpose is to evolve human into the being with the same size as the Earth through the Earth. Like this, evolution through Bon occurs in the same way as a child born from a mother becomes a mother.

Sim (心, the Mind)

The Mind (心) symbolizes the completion of earthly evolution. And it is human that is selected as the subject of this evolution. In the Cheon Bu Gyeong the Mind is not the purpose or result, but the process of following the brightness of the Sun to finish as InJungCheonJiIl (人中天地一). The difference between BonSim and InJungCheonJiIl (人中天地一) is due to the difference between SamGeuk and CheonJiIn. BonSim is CheonJiIn SamJae merged into one, and InJungCheonJiIl (人中天地一) is SamGeuk merged into one. SamGeuk created CheonJiIn at the one Geuk of SamGeuk (three Geuks) by replicating the property of SamGeuk. In this process human was selected, and is completed when he has the

Mind through the process of SaengChilPalGu (生七八九). This is CheonJiIn (the sky, the earth, human) merged into one. And it means that human becomes a state of one Geuk of SamGeuk. In this state, if human follows the brightness of the Sun, the other two Geuks of the SamGeuk merge again into one inside human. It is InJungCheonJiIl (人中天地一). The cosmos makes the Earth not lose its purpose of existence through the Sun. And the Earth makes human arrive at the finish by completing human with BonSim. Thus, the evolutionary turning point of the Earth and the cosmos is human having the Mind as Bon, and this is the reason why human must evolve to have the Mind. This principle of the Cheon Bu Gyeong remains in the Do Deok Gyeong (道德經, Tao Te Ching in Chinese) as Constantly Continuing Do (常道) and Do (道), and this is the reason that the people who have become Gods say that Do (道) is the Mind.

The obligation as a people of the descendants from the sky (天孫民族)

The obligation as a people of the descendants from the sky (天孫民族) is to be the inheritors of the cosmic principle, and to tell the world at the appropriate time that all the people are the descendants of the sky. What has been passed down is the cosmic principle of the human emergence on the Earth, and the Cheon Bu Gyeong is the scripture that contains the principle. And HongIkInGan (弘益人間) is doing its role by revealing the principle to the world at the appropriate time. There needs to be a clear understanding of HongIkInGan (弘益人間) in order to fulfill the obligation as a people of the descendants from the sky. HongIkInGan (弘益人間) has a meaning not only as a role, 'benefiting humans far and wide', but also as a being, 'people who benefit humans far and wide'. In the Cheon Bu Gyeong HongIkInGan (弘益人間) is the existential symbol of human with BonSim, and the role of HongIkInGan (弘益人間) is to make other people have BonSim.

The world that is filled with HongIkInGan (弘益人間) with BonSim (本心) is IHwaSeGye (理化世界). This is a condition where all humans are saints with the Mind and prepared to become Gods pursuing the brightness. In order for human to reach the condition, the Cheon Bu Gyeong which is the golden rule of ancient mentality must be passed down and be known around the world.

And this is the obligation of a people of the descendants from the sky. Like this, IHwaSeGye (理化世界) filled with HongIkInGan (弘益人間) is the image of SinSi (神市) before the Gojoseon era (古朝鮮), established by HwanWoong (桓雄), son of Hwanin (桓因), who came down from the sky with a group of people. The whole nation experienced the SinSi and continue the tradition up to the present, so Koreans are called a people of the descendants from the sky. The proof is the Cheon Bu Gyeong. The Cheon Bu Gyeong is the root of HongIkInGan (弘益人間), IHwaSeGye (理化世界) and SamGyoHoeTong (三敎會通, intermixture of three religions). They are the symbols for mentality of ancient times when humans and the sky were linked.

Various peoples live on the Earth with their own traditions and each people have their own position on the sky. For the Jews, it is 'the nation of people chosen by God'. For the Chinese, it is 'the country ruled by emperor, son of the sky'. The Egyptians have called it 'the nation ruled by Son of the Sun'. In this way, 'people chosen by the sky' or 'people ruled by son of the sky' is a usual position on the relationship between human and the sky. Koreans are the only people on the Earth who have the tradition of descendants from the sky which is to say that 'all the people are the descendants from the sky'. People of the descendants from the sky is the ethnic Korean mentality which means that people come from the sky to live on the Earth and then go back to the sky. This exactly corresponds to the principle of cosmic evolution in the Cheon Bu Gyeong. And this is the reason and purpose behind keeping existential purity symbolized as 'single-race nation (單一民族, racially homogeneous nation)' and 'white-clad race (白衣民族)' for a long time.

The appearance of the Cheon Bu Gyeong around a century ago is an indication that it is now the time to complete the forgotten obligation of the descendants from the sky. This obligation is to present the path of pursuing the sky to the people trapped inside the world. That is the teachings of the Cheon Bu Gyeong as follows. 'SamGeuk created CheonJiIn and selected human to be an earthly being. And human made and ran the world to correspond to the purpose of the sky.' As for the existence it is returning to HongIkInGan (弘益人間), and as for the world it is the process of going forth to IHwaSeGye (理化世界). In order for humans to return to HongIkInGan (弘益人間), they must do BanBonHwanWon (返本還原, returning to clean and pure natural state) going through the stages of ManWangManRae (萬往萬來), YongByeonBuDongBon (用變不動本) and BonSim (本心). This is the process where human consciousness returns from the world to human and then becomes HongIkInGan (弘益人間) by combining CheonJiIn. Only then humans can reach InJungCheonJiIl (人中天地一) where SamGeuk (三極, three Geuks) are merged and return to the sky. For this, it is the obligation of the descendants from the sky to help humans change by themselves the human world into SinSi (神市) that is IHwaSeGye (理化世界) filled with HongIkInGhan.

The founding principle and ruling ideology of Korea is the cosmic evolutionary principle of HongIkInGan (弘益人間) and JaeSeIHwa (在世理化). The former is a human evolution, and the latter is an evolution of the world. Through the combination of these two evolutions, SinSi (神市) is founded and the purpose of God coming down from the sky to the Earth is fulfilled. And then humans also can return to the sky as Gods. With passing down this mentality, the Koreans became the only people who say InNaeCheon (人乃天) which means 'human is the sky'. It means that human can return to the sky if they can resolve 'relation (因緣)' and ' causality (因果)' by their freedom, spontaneous will planted by the cosmos for humans to continue the evolutionary process. Humans return to the sky because humans are the children of the sky, and this is why Koreas call the national foundation day as 'the day when the sky opened (開天節)'.

The usage of the Cheon Bu Gyeong

The only way to overcome the relativity and the limit of consciousness trapped in the world is to realize the existence of human by the Mind. For this reason the Cheon Bu Gyeong shows a phased human character, BonSim (本心) and InJungCheonJiIl (人中天地一). The conversion of consciousness like this will hatch humans staying inside the egg, the Earth. The cosmos will make humans walk the path to become Gods for the original purpose of the cosmos. The purpose of this path is not Do (道, Tao in Chinese), the Mind but to reach Constantly Continuing Do (常道) which is Mu starting from Do (道), the Mind. This is the path that Buddha, Jesus and Lao

Tzu showed. Humans should not pursue the faith of the world, but follow their path as exactly as they walked it. The Cheon Bu Gyeong is the map which shows the whole path, and it can be used as the brightness that helps human change the root of study and hatch out of the eggs.

The Cheon Bu Gyeong contains the reason why humans naturally walk the path. For this purpose, the human existence must be changed into what continues constantly (常) from without what continues constantly (無常). Like this it is the role of God to pull out the root of wrong human consciousness. The Cheon Bu Gyeong, which has perfectly captured the principle of this cosmic divinity, can become an excellent assistant for human to cross the border of the world and restore the original existence. Deok (德, Te in Chinese) is the human nature planted by the Earth for human not to stray from the path of evolution. It is the combination of cosmic divinity, Do (道) and nature of the Earth, Deok (德) that exists as DoDeok (道德, Tao Te in Chinese) for human. This means that humans must realize that they are created on the Earth not just for the repetition of life and death. Therefore, humans have to be able to use the Cheon

Bu Gyeong to create a human-centered world in which humans coexist and live together as an independent human.

Humans have paid enough fees for thousands of years because they have been on the wrong path. Now there is a need for education to create a world suitable for human, rather than to make humans fit the orders of the world. The Cheon Bu Gyeong contains in abundance both what humans have to learn as well as the ways of learning. The starting point is knowing that CheonJiIn (天地人) is made for the need of SamGeuk, and the world made by human is nothing more than patterns painted on the CheonJiIn. The Cheon Bu Gyeong is a scripture prepared for all human. So it says that the essence of God and human is the same in the manner free from all civilizations and religions on the Earth. It is to reclaim the grounds on which human is existentially self-reliant. And it is the reason why we have to read the Cheon Bu Gyeong now.

Through the principle that binds humans and the cosmos together, conflicts from religions, races, civilizations, ideologies and cultures can be controlled.

Thus the Cheon Bu Gyeong is an open source provided by the cosmos for humans to realize that they are cosmic beings that live following the Mind. The Earth was created by this principle and materials and the same way was used again to create humans. Open consciousness of human could create civilizations, religions, cultures, and knowledge of the world. Through the Cheon Bu Gyeong, humans must recover the original vitality and find the original form of humans who were special beings with their infinite creativity. Korea is the country with unlimited resources, the Mind and the source of wealth, the mentality of HongIkInGan (弘益人間). If Koreans realize the fact and come to be able to share the tradition with other countries for IHwaSeGye (理化世界), the principle and ideological heritage of the Cheon Bu Gyeong will become a powerful force to protect humans and brighten the future. The Cheon Bu Gyeong is the true heritage that can correctly establish historical view and cultural tradition of Korea. If Koreans realize this by themselves, they can achieve a new era that not a religion, but a single nation becomes a historical standard throughout the whole mankind.

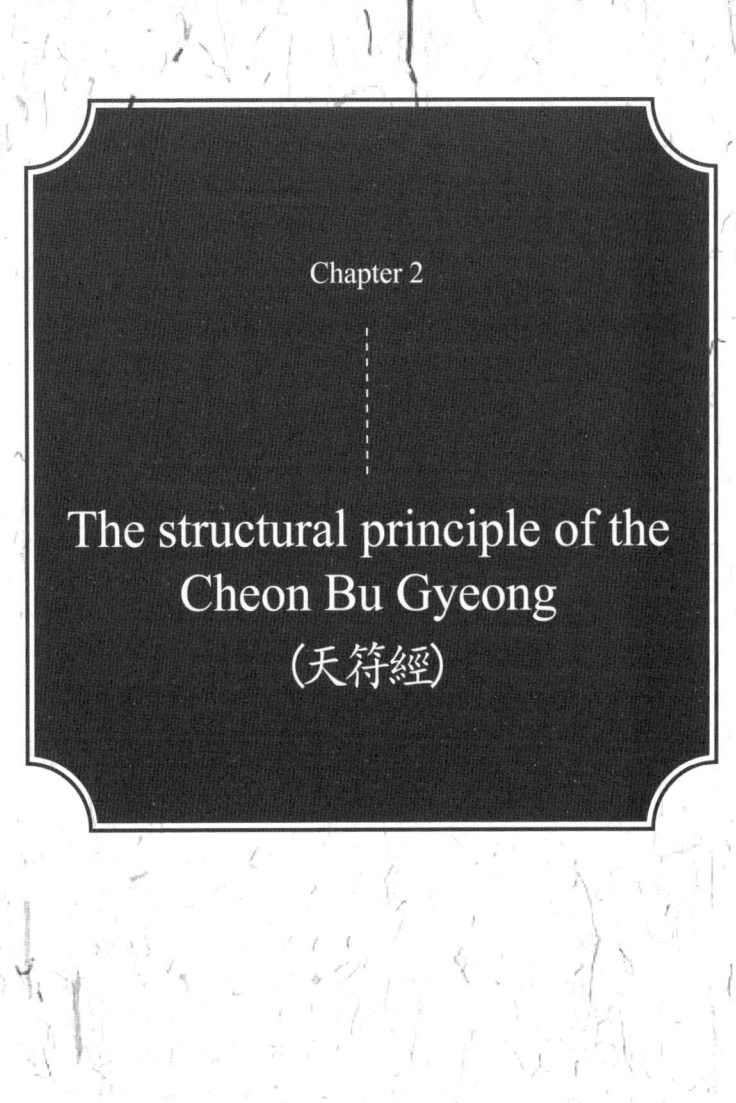

Chapter 2

The structural principle of the Cheon Bu Gyeong
(天符經)

天 符 經 Cheon Bu Gyeong

一	始	無	始	一	析	三	極	無
Il	Si	Mu	Si	Il	Seok	Sam	Geuk	Mu

盡	本	天	一	一	地	一	二	人
Jin	Bon	Cheon	Il	Il	Ji	Il	I	In

一	三	一	積	十	鉅	無	櫃	化
Il	Sam	Il	Jeok	Sip	Geo	Mu	Gwe	Hwa

三	天	二	三	地	二	三	人	二
Sam	Cheon	I	Sam	Ji	I	Sam	In	I

三	大	三	合	六	生	七	八	九
Sam	Dae	Sam	Hap	Yuk	Saeng	Chil	Pal	Gu

運	三	四	成	環	五	七	一	妙
Un	Sam	Sa	Seong	Hwan	O	Chil	Il	Myo

衍	萬	往	萬	來	用	變	不	動
Yeon	Man	Wang	Man	Rae	Yong	Byeon	Bu	Dong

本	本	心	本	太	陽	昂	明	人
Bon	Bon	Sim	Bon	Tae	Yang	Ang	Myeong	In

中	天	地	一	一	終	無	終	一
Jung	Cheon	Ji	Il	Il	Jong	Mu	Jong	Il

天 Cheon : the sky / 符 Bu : correspond to, be in accordance with / 經 Gyeong : scripture, sacred book / 一 Il : One / 始 Si : begin / 無 Mu : the state before the Big Bang, zero, nothing, extinct / 析 Seok : divide / 三 Sam : Three / 極 Geuk : pole / 盡 Jin : exhaust / 本 Bon : the Root / 二 I : Two / 地 Ji : the Earth, earth / 人 In : human / 積 Jeok : accumulate / 十 Sip : Ten / 鉅 Geo : expand / 櫃(匱) Gwe : box, body / 化 Hwa : become / 大 Dae : expand, raise / 合 Hap : combine / 六 Yuk : Six / 生 Saeng : live / 七 Chil : Seven / 八 Pal : Eight / 九 Gu : Nine / 運 Un : operate / 四 Sa : Four / 成 Seong : complete / 環 Hwan : circulate, repeat / 五 O : Five / 妙 Myo : mysterious / 衍 Yeon : flow / 萬 Man : Ten thousand / 往 Wang : go / 來 Rae : come / 用 Yong : use, usage / 變 Byeon : change / 不 Bu : not / 動 Dong : move / 心 Sim : the Mind / 太陽 Taeyang : the sun / 昂 Ang : follow / 明 Myeong : the brightness / 中 Jung : in, center / 終 Jong : finish

The principle of a cosmic evolutionary path walked by God
Cheon Bu Gyeong (天符經)

The structural principle of the Cheon Bu Gyeong
(天符經)

The Cheon Bu Gyeong is a short scripture composed of only 81 letters. However its name 'Cheon Bu (天符, Correspond to the sky)' shows that it contains a principle corresponding to the sky. The sky is explained to be Mu (無, the state before the Big Bang, zero, nothing, extinct) and Bon (本, the Root) that creates beings. And the beings created from the Mu are main agents of the correspondence. Based on this, the sky is classified into the universe and the Earth according to the Mu and the beings that must correspond to them are the Earth and human each. The sky of human is the Mu of the Earth, the sky of the Earth is the Mu of the universe and the sky of the universe is the Absolute Mu. Following this is 'Cheon Bu (天符)' which means 'corresponding to the sky.' Humans lost their existence recognition ability, so it is difficult for them to interpret Mu and Bon. Hence, The Cheon

Bu Gyeong is difficult for them to understand in spite of its simplicity and perspicuity. This led to needs for the appropriate standard to read the Cheon Bu Gyeong. Among the various methods, the most appropriate one is to follow the order of the original text arranged by the principle corresponding to the sky.

The Cheon Bu Kyung contains everything it wants to impart in the name 'Cheon Bu' and 81 letters. Therefore the order of arrangement and structure in accordance with the purpose of the sky are important tools to the interpretation system. The standard of the sky is Mu. The Earth creates human through the role in accordance with the sky and human must walk the path of 'SaengChilPalGu (生七八九)' which corresponds to the purpose of the universe. The sky of the Cheon Bu Kyung is not Cheon (the sky) of 'CheonJiIn (天地人, the sky, the Earth and human)'. It is the sky as the cosmic principle that CheonJiIn, the earthly time and space must corresponds to. Through this, it tries to teach that human has the existential responsibility to trace the sky. The process is to follow the sun after tracing back to CheonJiIn and SamGeuk (三極). So the process becomes an evolution.

In the Cheon Bu Gyeong, SamGeuk and CheonJiIn are clearly distinguished and used in separate ways. CheonJiIn is the earthly beings, time and space created by SamGeuk which is Bon with the property of SamGeuk for the purpose of Cheon Bu. CheonJiIn is made by replicating SamGeuk to be the base and materials for the operation of the Earth, so it becomes SamJae (三才). For this reason, the order of the scripture is as follows. Firstly, the Earth begins as MuSiIl (無始一) and then SamGeuk, Bon of the Earth is created in the Earth of MuSiIl. After that CheonJiIn settles down and human is selected among all creation. Lastly human finishes as MuJongIl (無終一). The contents of the Cheon Bu Kyung can be divided into 9 verses. These 9 verses are connected through a single operating principle and each verse can be interpreted independently in itself.

The operating principle of the Cheon Bu Gyeong is UnSam (運三) and SaSeong (四成). The operation of the Cheon Bu Kyung can be classified into 2 parts on the basis of Yuk (Six) which is placed at the center of 81 letters. The former is that the earth is created and then human is selected in consequence of the structural operation of CheonJiIn. The latter is that human goes through IlMyoYeon (一妙衍) and then becomes MuJongIl (無終一). The principle of UnSam (運三) and SaSeong (四成) is applied to all these operations and explains that human evolution is by the purpose of the sky. Through the existential characteristics of the sky and Mu, the Cheon Bu Gyeong explains about the principle of a cosmic evolutionary path into God walked by human. Therefore, for human the structure of the Cheon Bu Gyeong is as follows. The Earth which has begun from Mu as Mu creates CheonJi (天地) and all creation with SamGeuk, and selects human among them to be the being in accordance with the sky, and then makes human finish through the repeated operation and circulation. The principle of the Cheon Bu Gyeong which begins with 'IlSi (一始)' and finishes with 'MuJongIl (無終一)' let us know that everything from the universe to human is connected through the same principle and existence.

Chapter 3

Explanations of the original text of the Cheon Bu Gyeong

Cheon Bu Gyeong

IlSiMuSiIl (一始無始一),
One begins and it begins from Mu
SeokSamGeuk (析三極),
Divided into SamGeuk (Three Geuks)
MuJinBon (無盡本).
An inexhaustible Bon (the Root).

CheonIlIl, JiIlI, InIlSam (天一一, 地一二, 人一三).
Cheon is Il (One), Ji is I (Two) and In is Sam (Three) in the first operation.

IlJeokSipGeo (一積十鉅),
Accumulated One by One expands up to Sip (Ten)
MuGweHwaSam (無櫃化三).
When Gwe is extinct, it becomes Sam (Three).

CheonISam, JiISam, InISam (天二三, 地二三, 人二三).
Cheon is Sam (Three), Ji is Sam (Three) and In is Sam (Three) as well in the second operation.

DaeSamHapYuk (大三合六),
Sam (Three) is expanded and combined into Yuk (Six)
SaengChilPalGu (生七八九).
To be born as Chil (Seven), Pal (Eight) and Gu (Nine).

UnSam (運三),
The principle of operation is Sam (Three)

SaSeong (四成),
The principle of completion is Sa (Four)
HwanOChil (環五七).
The principle of circulation is O (Five) and Chil (Seven).

IlMyoYeon (一妙衍),
The flow of Il (One) is mysterious
ManWangManRae (萬往萬來),
Even though it comes and goes ten thousand times
YongByeonBuDongBon (用變不動本).
Usage changes but Bon does not move.

BonSim (本心),
Bon is Sim (the Mind)
BonTaeYangAngMyeong (本太陽昂明),
When looking up to Bon, the brightness of the Sun
InJungCheonJiIl (人中天地一).
Cheon and Ji becomes Il (One) inside In (Human).

IlJongMuJongIl (一終無終一).
Il (One) finishes and it finishes as Mu.

天 Cheon : the sky / 符 Bu : correspond to, be in accordance with / 經 Gyeong : scripture, sacred book / 一 Il : One / 始 Si : begin / 無 Mu : the state before the Big Bang, zero, nothing, extinct / 析 Seok : divide / 三 Sam : Three / 極 Geuk : pole / 盡 Jin : exhaust / 本 Bon : the Root / 二 I : Two / 地 Ji : the Earth, earth / 人 In : human / 積 Jeok : accumulate / 十 Sip : Ten / 鉅 Geo : expand / 櫃(匱) Gwe : box, body / 化 Hwa : become / 大 Dae : expand, raise / 合 Hap : combine / 六 Yuk : Six / 生 Saeng : live / 七 Chil : Seven / 八 Pal : Eight / 九 Gu : Nine / 運 Un : operate / 四 Sa : Four / 成 Seong : complete / 環 Hwan : circulate, repeat / 五 O : Five / 妙 Myo : mysterious / 衍 Yeon : flow / 萬 Man : Ten thousand / 往 Wang : go / 來 Rae : come / 用 Yong : use, usage / 變 Byeon : change / 不 Bu : not / 動 Dong : move / 心 Sim : the Mind / 太陽 Taeyang : the sun / 昂 Ang : follow / 明 Myeong : the brightness / 中 Jung : in, center / 終 Jong : finish

Verse 1

IlSiMuSiIl (一始無始一),

One begins and it begins from Mu

SeokSamGeuk (析三極),

Divided into SamGeuk (Three Geuks)

MuJinBon (無盡本).

An inexhaustible Bon (the Root).

一 Il : One / 始 Si : begin / 無 Mu : the state before the Big Bang, zero, nothing, extinct / 始 Si : begin / 一 Il : One
析 Seok : divide / 三 Sam : Three / 極 Geuk : pole
無 Mu : the state before the Big Bang, zero, nothing, extinct / 盡 Jin : exhaust / 本 Bon : the Root

IlSiMuSill (一始無始一),
One begins and it begins from Mu

'One begins (一始)' means that 'a certain being' emerges for the first time. Something that had never existed comes into existence. 'A being that has never existed' emerges into 'a time and space that has never existed'. So the place where One begins is called Mu. This is the process that 'a certain being' called the cosmos emerges into a state of Mu, and in the Mu space of the cosmos, the Earth, 'a being that has never existed' emerges and settles down. All creation is also created by the same principle, and this is the principle that the beginning (始) is connected with the being born (生). The Cheon Bu Gyeong begins with MuSiIl (無始一) and establishes the fact that the beginning of 'a certain being' relies on Mu, and the state of it is Mu. IlSiMuSiIl (一始無始一) shows the principle that Mu is expanded and compressed through the connection of the cosmos to the Earth, and the Earth to humans. Through this it teaches that humans must return to the state of cosmic Mu and shows the way how to return.

All things such as the cosmos, the Earth, and all creation began from Mu. After the beginning of the cosmos from the Absolute Mu (絶代無), the Earth and all creation began sequentially. So the cosmos, the Earth, and all creation begin and exist in reliance on the higher level of Mu which is the root of their Mu. The Mu of IlSiMuSiIl (一始無始一) implies both 'the place' and 'the time' of the beginning simultaneously. In other words, it contains the meaning that One begins from Mu and the state of One when it begins is Mu. Through IlSiMuSiIl (一始無始一) coming out of Mu (無), the Mu of MuJongIl (無終一) and the Mu that is begun (一始) become connected in meaning. Like this, the cosmos, the Earth, and all creation are Mu connected through Mu. So the circulation and the finish can occur according to the purpose. The Cheon Bu Gyeong attempts to show the process that a being that began from Mu finishes as Mu. This process is expanding and compressing one material under the principle corresponding to one purpose. The process flows with the repetition of selection and concentration, so it becomes an evolution.

It is the Absolute Mu that created the time and space of the cosmos as well as all creation in it. This is possible because the Absolute Mu is a being, time and space at the same time. And this image is a symbol of God. And the existence of the Absolute Mu is equal to that of the MuJongIl (無終一) of IlJongMuJongIl (一終無終一) with the exception of size. This is important to understand the Cheon Bu Gyeong. IlSiMuSiIl (一始無始一) implies that the Absolute Mu creates a womb, the Earth. And human is a fetus of the Absolute Mu in it. Through the evolutionary process, the fetus is born as God in the same condition as the Absolute Mu and then becomes the Absolute Mu through the life as God in the cosmos. This process is the original purpose of human evolution. For this reason, it is said that 'human resembles God' or 'human is the sky (人乃天)'. And this is why Koreans who are based on InNaeCheon (人乃天, human is the sky) can be called a people of the descendants from the sky. So the evolution of human proceeds like this; to create the Mind and then go over to the cosmos by having Mu within the Mind. That is why Yuk (Six) which is the symbol of human is placed at the center of eighty-one letters of the Cheon Bu Gyeong. This is the reason why human whose purpose is not evolution but the life in the world can never be free.

It is for evolution that the Absolute Mu requires phased bases and beings. Mu cannot evolve in itself. So it is necessary to create beings suitable for evolution by phased compression. The Cheon Bu Gyeong tries to inform that the cosmos and the Earth are selected as the bases and humans as the beings for evolution. For this, the first sentence IlSiMuSiIl (一始無始一) shows the time and space of Mu and the state of independence. The last sentence IlJongMuJongIl (一終無終一) shows the state of finish and self-reliance. This is why the meaning of Mu varies between IlSiMuSiIl (一始無始一) and IlJongMuJongIl (一終無終一) from 'a being as time and space' to 'What is a being, time and space at once'. Through this the Cheon Bu Gyeong shows that the purpose of Mu is to go from IlSi (一始, the beginning of One) to IlJong (一終, the finish of One). And it is the guidebook that teaches the role of human and the process how human was selected as a being suitable for the purpose by the principle of life. The big loop between IlSiMuSiIl (一始無始一) and IlJongMuJongIl (一終無終一) connects Mu of the Earth, the sky of human, and Mu of the cosmos, the sky of the Earth through the sky which is the phased purpose of human. And it explains that the principle and purpose of the cosmic operation lie in evolution. The small loop between life and circulation shows the changes and ways of existences in the evolutionary process through the existence of the Mu separated from the cosmos. IlSiMuSiIl (一始無始一) which means that One begins from Mu in a state of Mu is the basic premise of this.

The evolution of Mu is that a being based on Mu becomes the same state as the Mu. And the Cheon Bu Gyeong shows that it is the reason for the existence of the cosmos. The principle of the cosmos connects beings and Mu through the process where what has never existed begins and gets born. For this reason, the result of finish (終) or stop (死=己) is nothing but Mu. The beginning of One (一始) is the beginning of cosmic causality based on the natural way of Mu. The Earth also operates creating the natural way and causality of the earthly Mu to correspond to the cosmic purpose. IlSiMuSill (一始無始一) contains the law between times and spaces with the meaning of the sentence that 'One begins from Mu' and 'it begins as Mu'. MuSill (無始一) shows that IlSi (一始) is the beginning of new Mu separated from Mu. IlSiMuSill (一始無始一) is the same state of the cosmos as it emerged first but not spread yet. It is by going through this process that the Mu and the beings of the cosmos can share the same character, purpose and operating principle. The Cheon Bu Gyeong shows that the beginning of One (一始) is the generative principle of the cosmos that One begins from Mu as Mu. The principle is also applied to the Earth and all creation, by which human emerged. Therefore, IlSiMuSill (一始無始一) is that One becomes independent as Mu. And it shows that the process is required for what has begun as Mu to become self-reliant. This way of independence and self-reliance is the root of cosmic evolution.

The cosmos created the Earth, a star with a purpose. And the Earth created all creation in order to correspond to the purpose of the cosmos, and selected human as a suitable being among them. Human selected as the subject of evolution at the end of the cosmic differentiation walks the path of WonSiBanBon (原始返本). It is the process of phased return to the Earth which is the sky of human and finally to the Mu of the cosmos. The human which has gone through this process evolves into the state of what is a being, time and space at once, the original form of Mu unlike the Earth, a being of time and space. This is the difference between the cosmos and the Earth, and the state is the original form of the Absolute Mu. Like this, the basic way of the cosmic evolution is not different from the principle of human reproduction. It is because the cosmos was created to evolve that human becomes

Mu with existence and traces back to the earthly Mu and then to the cosmic Mu. And it is the Cheon Bu Gyeong that shows this principle and purpose through IlSiMuSiIl (一始無始一) and IlJongMuJongIl (一終無終一). Through this process human evolves into the form of God and exists in a state of MuJongIl (無終一). The cosmos, the Earth, and human all have begun from Mu and the principle of their finish is the same. And human is the existential connection link among them. For human, IlSiMuSiIl (一始無始一) is the beginning of evolution by the purpose of the cosmos. Human is a being created to pursue the finish as Mu while going through the process of being operated, completed and circulated in a time and space. This process persists from all creation to human and from the Earth to the cosmos. So it is the evolution as the principle corresponding to the cosmos, the sky (天).

IlSiMuSiIl (一始無始一) is a beginning of evolution, and IlJongMuJongIl (一終無終一) symbolizes an emergence of a new being after the completion of the evolutionary process. This makes the difference between the Mu of IlSiMuSiIl (一始無始一) and the Mu of IlJongMuJongIl (一終無終一). As the Cheon Bu Gyeong teaches, human must live for the finish as human rather than for human life.

For this, human needs to establish his position on Mu. We must accept the reason why the Absolute Mu created the cosmos, the Earth, and human, and why each of them exists. This is the backbone of the InNaeCheon (人乃天, Human is the sky) ideology. Through IlSiMuSiIl (一始無始一), we can know that all the Ones such as the cosmos, the Earth, and human have the same root created from Mu. And human was selected to be the being of cosmic evolution to bear fruits through this root. 'What has begun is in a state of Mu' means that it becomes completely independent and indicates the existence with one purpose. IlSiMuSiIl (一始無始一) means that all creation of the cosmos and the Earth carries the unity through the same purpose, and clarifies that the purpose is the evolutionary path with the connection of IlJongMuJongIl (一終無終一). It is a principle that One has its own path and purpose, and becomes independent and then self-reliant as an existence of One. We must realize the reason why the Earth selected a being among all creation for evolution and why human was selected as the being. Through this, IlSiMuSiIl (一始無始一) implies that human must walk the path in accordance with that.

SeokSamGeuk (析三極),

Divided into SamGeuk (Three Geuks)

The newly created One is in an entire lump state of Mu. SeokSamGeuk (析三極) is the state in which the Earth begins to change from MuSiIl (無始一) into the time and space in accordance with the purpose of the cosmos. Through SeokSamGeuk (析三極), the Earth is divided from a state of Mu into three properties, and this state is SamGeuk (三極) which is the Bon of the Earth. Through this it can be known that the existence of the Earth is time and space. The Earth which is only time and space of Mu creates CheonJiIn (天地人) with SamGeuk to have beings. SamGeuk, which is Mu as well as Bon, is MuJinBon (無盡本) because it operates CheonJiIn as time and space, and that is why SamGeuk becomes the standard of changes and evolutions on the Earth. A being continues its existence as long as this Bon lasts. It is also the same principle by which Bon of human continues if he becomes BuDongBon (不動本). Like this, SeokSamGeuk (析三極) is a state where one Mu carries three different properties. The cosmos was also unfolded after the lumped process like SeokSamGeuk (析三極) at the beginning from Mu. For this reason, the huge cosmos can operate according to the Bon and principle in accordance with the purpose. Therefore, MuSiIl (無始一) and SeokSamGeuk (析三極) is Bon as well as the Earth in a state of Mu. And CheonJiIn and human is operation as well as the Earth in a state of having beings on it. It is possible because the Earth has the fixedness as a state of One and the motility by the division into three Geuks.

As the Earth gains three kinds of properties through SeokSamGeuk (析三極), it becomes a separate time and space from the cosmos. Three properties divided by SeokSamGeuk (析三極) act as the Bon of everything on the Earth, so they are called SamGeuk (三極). With SamGeuk, the base of the earthly Mu separated from the cosmic Mu becomes ready. CheonJiIn (天地人) is created by SamGeuk and is the base for the operation corresponding to the cosmic purpose, so it is called SamJae (三才) to distinguish from SamGeuk. The earthly evolution proceeds centered on beings through the process of UnSam (運三) where SamJae are created and operated. The cosmos has three Geuks (極) that are expanding space from the starting point to the target point, and multiple times for the stars. On the other hand, the Earth has only limited space and uniform time. That is the difference between them. However, there is also a similarity between the cosmos and the Earth. Both of them operate time and space with their own beings, stars and humans each, by SamGeuk which are three Geuks in a state of Mu. In this way, the difference in the existence style and the role between the cosmos and the Earth is the conceptual difference between the SamGeuk and SamJae. SamGeuk is the cosmic property, Mu, and is like the lumped state before the big bang. SamJae is like the state where stars are created and operated after expansion due to the big bang.

SamGeuk carries out the role corresponding to the cosmic purpose by operating SamJae. SeokSamGeuk (析三極) is the same state as MuSilIl (無始一) in the sense that there are no beings. It is just separated as time and space of Mu that keeps exactly the property of the cosmos. In that state, SamGeuk creates CheonJiIn (天地人) SamJae, and becomes the Bon (本) of the earthly time and space operated by CheonJiIn. Like this, SeokSamGeuk (析三極) is that the Earth separated with the materials of the cosmos, Mu, begins the evolution in accordance with the purpose of the cosmos. It is the

Mu as a border that makes the Earth a separate time and space, the Mu as the materials of the cosmos, and the Mu as a space in motion. Therefore, SamGeuk is still in a state of Mu, and this process is the same as the creation of the cosmos. This property of SamGeuk changes into CheonJiIn through the process of UnSam (運三). The Mu as a border that makes the Earth a separate time and space becomes the sky. The Mu as the materials of the cosmos becomes land and all creation and then they are placed in the gap (間), the Mu as a space in motion. CheonJiIn is created and operated in the gap (間) which is a Geuk of SamGeuk (Three Geuks). The Mu of the Earth was divided in a state of Mu, so CheonJiIn could be created. Through SeokSamGeuk (析三極) the Earth has changed into the star which plays a role to correspond to the purpose of the cosmos.

SeokSamGeuk (析三極) is the starting point of the evolutionary process of the Earth in accordance with the purpose of the cosmos. And it is Bon which made the base for operation and all creation exist. SamGeuk which has settled as Bon creates CheonJiIn SamJae through UnSam and gives each of them its own role. It is through the process of SeokSamGeuk (析三極) that a time and space operated by CheonJiIn comes to be on the Earth. SamGeuk symbolizes the cosmic time and space which is Mu, and SamJae is the earthly time and space centered on beings. It is through SeokSamGeuk (析三極) that the time and Mu of the cosmos is grafted onto the Earth in an appropriate form, and the earthly time and space operates in accordance with the purpose of the cosmos. SamGeuk is like the state of Mu where there are no stars in the cosmos. It creates and operates SamJae with the cosmic property which creates and operates stars from Mu. For the Earth of MuSilIl (無始一), Bon is begun from SeokSamGeuk (析三極) and SamJae is created from the Bon, SamGeuk. And human makes the completion corresponding to the cosmic purpose in the circulation process of all creation.

The Cheon Bu Gyeong distinguishes SamGeuk which is Mu and CheonJiIn which is beings, time and space at once. For this reason, there is a need to clearly separate SeokSamGeuk (析三極) for SamGeuk from the process of UnSam for CheonJiIn. SeokSamGeuk (析三極) is the process where the Earth has its separate Bon from the cosmos. On the other hand, UnSam is the process of operating the earthly evolution by making the structure of CheonJiIn with Bon. Among UnSam (運三), 1 Un (1運) is the beginning (生) of CheonJiIn, the separate beings, time and space of the Earth, 2 Un (2運) is the circulation (環) of the CheonJiIn in a connected state of One, and 3 Un (3運) is the completion (成) process centered on the evolution of human selected by the Earth for the finish (終). The cosmos expects human to evolve into Mu, a being made through merging CheonJiIn and SamGeuk into one.

The cosmos has identical Mu and multiple and complex time. In this state, the purpose of the cosmos begun as One from the Absolute Mu (絶代無) cannot be achieved. So, the cosmos assigns each role to its identical Mu by operating time independently. This is the reason why the Earth was created. And SeokSamGeuk (析三極) symbolizes that the Earth begins an independent operation for the role assigned to the Mu. Through this, the earthly time and space is created in the cosmos and operated in a separate state with being connected to the cosmos. So, SeokSamGeuk (析三極) is the process where the structure and time appropriate to the cosmic purpose are established on the Earth. The independence of time creates the earthly change, and it becomes the evolution connected to the time of the cosmos. For this, the Earth changes itself through SeokSamGeuk and UnSam to be suitable for its assigned role, and operates as a small cosmos placed in the process of the cosmic evolution. Like this, SamGeuk which manages the earthly evolution is clearly different from CheonJiIn SamJae which is operated as beings, time and space for the evolution.

SeokSamGeuk (析三極) is the primitive Earth in a state when SamGeuk (三極) is not yet divided. Therefore, it is possible for CheonJiIn created with the property of SamGeuk to operate being connected with one another. This point is the 'SamGeuk ideology (三極思想)' of the Cheon Bu Gyeong. As time passed, SamGeuk and CheonJiIn got mixed up as the same, hence human thoughts got trapped in CheonJiIn SamJae where UnSam occurs. Due to this, people just pursue the principle centered on the concept of changes such as TaeGeuk (太極) and EumYang (陰陽). They forgot the reason why the Earth and human exist and their purpose, the existential evolution. Therefore people became unable to understand the reason why CheonJiIn, namely time, space and human all happen in the space, the gap of

SamGeuk. And eventually the existential purpose and role of human have also been forgotten. The reason why Seok (析) is used rather than Bun (分) in SeokSamGeuk (析三極) is to show a difference in meaning. If Bun (分) is a separation into a completely separated individual, Seok (析) symbolizes a division in a state where they are still connected. So Seok (析) is used to show a state in which it is divided but still maintained as One. CheonJiIn is one interlinked with one another in a state of Bun (分), and SamGeuk is one in a state of Seok (析). The separated CheonJiIn can change and evolve because they are connected through SamGeuk.

MuJinBon (無盡本).
An inexhaustible Bon (the Root).

Bon is the earth in a state of SeokSamGeuk (析三極) with no beings on it. And It is in a state of Mu. The Earth gets independent Bon from the cosmos through SeokSamGeuk (析三極), which made the beginning and the being born possible on the Earth. Only when the Bon is inexhaustible, survival is possible. And only when it is unchanging, the operation according to the purpose is possible. Therefore, MuJinBon (無盡本) means that the Earth gained the characteristics of Bon, 'unchangingness' and 'inexhaustibleness'. And this makes the operation of CheonJiIn where the being born (生) and the going back (環) occur possible to continue constantly. MuJinBon is the characteristic of Bon that operates in accordance with the cosmic purpose, and the purpose is the existential evolution through CheonJiIn. Because Bon of the Earth is in a state of Mu, the size of IlJeokSipGeo (一積十鉅) of CheonJiIn becomes the same as that of the Earth. Also, the structural changes into CheonJiIn are the changes of Mu the earthly Bon has, so it does not affect Bon. It is just passing through structural changes on top of Bon to become suitable for the operation in accordance with the cosmic purpose.

In the process of the Earth gaining its Bon, Mu has settled as three Geuks, and the structure of CheonJiIn was made in one Geuk of them. MuJinBon means that the character of Bon is consistent throughout the process and the structure and purpose of the operation continues. This is connected with the characteristics of the evolutionary stages of BuDongBon (不動本), BonSim

(本心), and BonTaeYangAngMyeong (本太陽昂明). This shows that the Bon in each evolutionary stage neither changes nor becomes exhausted and stops. In this way, Bon of Chil (Seven/七), all creation, BuDongBon (不動本) of Pal (Eight/八), humans, and BonSim (本心) of Gu (Nine/九), the Self (我) function as MuJinBon in each stage. This also shows the higher level Bon needed for evolution. The reason that makes it possible is that Bon begins from the Mu of the cosmos. The earthly change is for the Earth filled with 'the visible' and 'the invisible' to operate internal evolution. It is Bon makes evolution by repeating Gwe (櫃) and Hwa (化) through CheonJiIn SamJae (三才). Therefore, Bon must have nothing to do with periodical situations or the number of beings on the Earth. MuJinBon explains that the earthly evolution can continue inexhaustibly because it is connected with the time and space of the cosmos. MuJinBon means that there will be no changes to the mass and the size of the Earth. And it informs that the time which is the root of Bon will continue without stopping.

Bon is created with the beginning of the earthly time. And in the process of the Bon creating the operational structure of CheonJiIn, the characteristic changes of

IlJeokSipGeo (一積十鉅) occurs. An evolutionary being, human is also the component of IlJeokSipGeo. And in that, the forms and contents of YongByeon (changes in usage, 用變) as well as the evolutionary stages are changed. Nevertheless, the fundamental value of One that has Bon in the cosmos is consistent, and its purpose also does not change. So it is MuJinBon. Through this it can be known that the role of the Earth and human according to the existential purpose will continue. The providence that moves the Earth and the cosmos is not different and the operation corresponding to each existential purposes and roles continues constantly. When human gains BonSim (本心) through the existential evolution according to this principle, human also becomes a state of MuJinBon, where human circulates as the self (我). It is the role of the earthly Bon to evolve all creation and human into beings circulating as the Self. And it can be known through IlJongMuJongIl (一終無終一) that this MuJinBon is for evolution which is the purpose of the cosmos. For this, the Earth creates CheonJiIn with its Bon, and continues constantly so that human can have the Mind as Bon. The Cheon Bu Gyeong shows through MuJinBon that Bon will continue the same process until humans finish their evolution. Because the Cheon

Bu Gyeong wants to inform that humans are on their evolutionary path without choice.

Verse 2

CheonIlIl, JiIlI, InIlSam (天一一, 地一二, 人一三).

Cheon is Il (One), Ji is I (Two) and In is Sam (Three) in the first operation.

天 Cheon : the sky / 一 Il : One / 一 Il : One
地 Ji : the Earth, earth / 一 Il : One / 二 I : Two
人 In : human / 一 Il : One / 三 Sam : Three

CheonIlIl, JiIlI, InIlSam (天一一, 地一二, 人一三).

Cheon is Il (One), Ji is I (Two) and In is Sam (Three) in the first operation.

'CheonIlIl JiIlI InIlSam (天一一 地一二 人一三)' is an explanation about 1 Un of UnSam (運三). 1 Un is the process where SamGeuk which is Bon creates CheonJiIn SamJae by the earthly time, and changes the property of SamGeuk into CheonJiIn. For this, 1 Un is a mixed state of the cosmic time symbolized by SamGeuk and the earthly time symbolized by SamJae. Through this process the Earth has the structure of a small cosmos, and after that it becomes bigger and combined in 2 Un to be able to fulfill its role. CheonJiIn is the base and subject of an operation that has been created in one Geuk of SamGeuk (Three Geuks). The Earthly time has created the independent time and space called CheonJiIn with the property of SamGeuk. This is the reason why the ChenJi (天地) of InJungCheonJiIl (人中天地一) that happens in BonSim (本心) is not ChenJi (天地) of CheonJiIn, but the other two Geuks of SamGeuk. This is because the purpose of the cosmos is to create a being of MuJongIl (無終一) with SamGeuk on the Earth. The directionality and circularity of time also shows that the purpose of the cosmos is evolution. 1 Un is the process of the earthly time gaining directionality in accord with that.

The reason that SamGeuk and SamJae coexist is because the Earth was selected to be a star for the cosmic purpose. Evolution cannot occur in a state of SamGeuk. It is because there are no beings to carry out evolution. Therefore, the Earth becomes equipped with the beings and the base for the time and space suitable for evolution through 1 Un. UnSam (運三) is the process of changing CheonJiIn into a suitable state for this, and selecting and evolving the existential subject. In 1 Un, all creation and the earthly time and space are created. In 2 Un, human is selected as a subject of existential evolution among all creation based on the stable time and space. In 3 Un, human goes through a self-evolutionary process. The purpose of operating CheonJiIn through UnSam is SaSeong (四成) of MuJongIl (無終一) and the way of human operation before his finish is HwanOChil (環五七). Like this, in 1 Un beings and the earthly time and space according to the cosmic purpose are created based on SamGeuk. Through this, the main agent of operating evolution is switched from the cosmos to the Earth.

1 Un is a state in which CheonJiIn carries both properties of SamGeuk and SamJae. It is both SamGeuk and SamJae at the same time, and is the process in which the cosmos and the Earth are connected through one single principle and purpose. There are no changes separated from the cosmos. The separated time and space, the Earth, gets to operate in accordance with the purpose of the cosmos through the connection process with the cosmos during 1 Un. All the processes and beings in the cosmos are connected through one single Mu, and the Mu of the Earth is also originally the Mu of the cosmos. Therefore, 1 Un is the process in which the operating structure of the Earth is changed from a state of SeokSamGeuk (析三極) into CheonJiIn (天地人). For this reason, CheonJiIn gains the property of SamGeuk, and operates in accordance with the purpose of the earthly Bon. As the time and space of the cosmos and the Earth are interlinked like this, the evolution according to the time of the cosmos begins on the Earth. This is possible because Bon, which is the main agent of operation, created CheonJiIn, the structure and subject of operation with Mu during 1 Un.

The Il (One) in the middle of CheonIlIl JiIlI InIlSam

(天一一地一二人一三) means that it is the first operation of UnSam (運三). Time for the earthly evolution is created during 1 Un, and according to the time the order of CheonJiIn and the standards of their roles are determined. The reason why time is created first is that no change or evolution can happen without time. Time makes changes and evolution proceeds following the flow of time. The time for this should be separated from the complex and various time of the cosmos. Accordingly, the cosmos gives each star the role of creating beings and separate time and space so that each of them evolves in accordance with the purpose of the cosmos. As a result, the time corresponding to the purpose appears and an independent operation from the cosmos takes place on the Earth. For this reason, the Cheon Bu Gyeong talks about the time and its directionality through the sequential arrangement of One (一), Two (二), and Three (三) in the 1 Un. The time starts from the earthly sky which is in contact with the cosmos and reaches down to the earthly beings.

The time makes each of the different cosmic properties of SamGeuk settle as the earthly form called CheonJiIn. The Earth is a star existing in the time and space of the cosmos and likewise CheonJiIn SamJae is a star created in the time and space of SamGeuk. The biggest difference between SamGeuk and CheonJiIn is in the existence. According to the order, the sky which separates the Earth from the cosmos is created first. And then the earth is created second through the substances being mixed under the sky. All creation appears thirdly in the gap (間) between them. This directionality of time shows that CheonJiIn was created for the beings, all creation. 1 Un is significant in that the base of evolution and various creations are created by the purpose of the cosmos. The reason why the letter, 'In (人, human)', is used in 1 Un without distinction from that of 2 Un is to symbolize that human comes out of all creation. Human is the result of the operation of the earthly evolution, and the Mind of human is the fruit of the evolution of CheonJiIn SamJae. InJungCheonJiIl (人中天地一) is that the remaining two Geuks of the SamGeuk which made CheonJiIn are kept in the Mind.

The Earth has been equipped with the functional structure of CheonJiJaYeon (天地自然, sky, earth and nature) through 1 Un in order to correspond to the purpose of the cosmos. Each component of CheonJiIn (天地人, the sky, the Earth and human) at this moment exists individually so it is only the structural completion. This is only a process of change in order to correspond to the purpose of the cosmos. There is no evolutionary operation. The base and subject (all creation) are made in 1 Un. And in 2 Un all creation gets bigger and combined into human with the operation according to the purpose. Therefore, the number that is gained through 1 Un is Sam (Three) because it is a separated Cheon, Ji and In, and through this it can be known that the purpose of 1 Un is Sam (Three), all creation. Stars which are beings in the flexible time and space of the cosmos cannot undergo existential evolution. On the other hand, CheonJi (the sky and the earth) of the Earth is fixed, and the roles of all creation which exists on it are fixed. Therefore evolution is possible on the Earth. This stability caused by having fixed time and space as well as beings makes evolution possible.

Verse 3

IlJeokSipGeo (一積十鉅),

Accumulated One by One expands up to Sip (Ten)

MuGweHwaSam (無櫃化三).

When Gwe is extinct, it becomes Sam (Three).

一 Il : One / 積 Jeok : accumulate / 十 Sip : Ten / 鉅 Geo : expand
無 Mu : the state before the Big Bang, zero, nothing, extinct / 櫃(匱) Gwe : box, body / 化 Hwa : become / 三 Sam : Three

IlJeokSipGeo (一積十鉅),
Accumulated One by One expands up to Sip (Ten)

IlJeokSipGeo (一積十鉅) shows the process where SamGeuk establishes CheonJiIn and shows the size that the Earth can expand to. Due to the expansion of IlJeokSipGeo occurring in the state of Mu, it continues until it becomes the same size as the entire Earth. Through this it is known that the size of the Earth is Sip (Ten). For this reason, IlJeokSipGeo becomes the standard of the evolutionary process of the Earth. Because the size of the Earth is Sip (Ten), the size of a being evolved through UnSam is Gu (Nine). IlJeok (一積) means that all creation has its role as an independent being. SipGeo (十鉅) expresses the state in which the independent beings mingle together. Therefore, IlJeokSipGeo also means that all creations are equal beings. The reason why IlJeokSipGeo appears before 2 Un is that IlJeokSipGeo is the result of 1 Un when CheonJiIn is structurally completed by expanding until it is in contact with the cosmos. Like this, if 1 Un is the straight flow of time that confirms the size and mass of the entire Earth, 2 Un is the circulation of time, so CheonJiIn can expand and be combined during 2 Un. The straight flow and the circulation of time becomes one through the process of expansion and combination of structuralized CheonJiIn, and then the evolution towards the cosmos becomes possible through the operation of 3 Un.

IlJeokSipGeo is the standard of the earthly evolution and the size of CheonJiIn created by SamGeuk. The Cheon Bu Gyeong teaches that there cannot be a being on the Earth that is bigger than Sip (Ten), the number of the Earth. This is the reason why the biggest number in the process of UnSam is Gu (Nine). If a being goes over Gu (Nine) then becomes the same number as the Earthly number, Sip (Ten), the being becomes a cosmic being out of the earthly limitation. Therefore, Sip (Ten) of IlJeokSipGeo is the base number of the Earth. And on the basis of Sip (Ten), evolutionary numbers of UnSam which are Il (One) through Gu (Nine) are accumulated and evolved according to the same standard. The number of SamGeuk becomes Sip (Ten) through IlJeokSipGeo and UnSam, and the number of CheonJiIn SamJae can be known to be Gu (Nine). Through this, BonSim which is the condition of CheonJiIn evolved into one becomes Gu (Nine), and InJungCheonJiIl (人中天地一) which is the condition of SamGeuk evolved into one becomes Sip

(Ten). IlJeokSipGeo is a state filled with the visible Mu and the invisible Mu of the Earth. And it is the same state as that of InJungCheonJiIl where human is filled with Mu and is in contact with the cosmos. IlJeokSipGeo of 1 Un which is a mixed state of SamGeuk and SamJae provides a basis for the Earth to be the time and space for evolution along with UnSam.

There is no concept of Young (zero) in the Cheon Bu Gyeong. This is because it is filling what already exists. By handling Sip (Ten) finished through IlJeokSipGeo, it shows that Young (zero) has the properties of Mu, that is 'the completion and the beginning'. Through this, it shows that Sip (Ten) which is the number of the Earth is a new starting point in the cosmos, and explains why human becomes a new being through MuJongIl when he finishes as One. The Cheon Bu Gyeong expresses the completed form of the Earth to be Geo (鉅). Geo (鉅) means the expansion (巨) of the entirety from Il (One) to Sip (Ten) and the unchangeable solidification (金) like steel through the establishment of the form and role. IlJeokSipGeo is the change of Bon which is SamGeuk into the foundation of CheonJiIn in the process of 1 Un. All creation operates in the way of MuGweHwaSam (無

櫃化三) on top of this foundation. With IlJeokSipGeo, the Cheon Bu Gyeong suggests that the number that human will carry is Sip (Ten), when he arrives at Gu (Nine) through UnSam and then finishes as One to become Mu of One. By presenting the size of the Earth and the standard of existence by IlJeokSipGeo, it is showing the reason why human who arrives at Gu (Nine) gets a chance to finish.

IlJeokSipGeo (一積十鉅) is a process for the earthly evolution. Through this, the standard of the evolution given by the cosmos to the Earth as well as the size and existence of the Earth in the cosmos are defined. In this way, the Cheon Bu Gyeong clearly defines itself as a scripture to pass down the cosmic evolution by showing the limitations of the earthly beings and the way how to overcome them. Sip (Ten) means that the Earth is the smallest evolutionary unit that occurs in the cosmos and is the starting point of the evolution. And it shows through MuJongIl that the finish of human as Sip (Ten) is to enter a bigger process of the cosmic evolution. Therefore, if human goes through the process of IlJeokSipGeo to become Sip (Ten), then the number behind it would start from SipIl (Eleven). If a being stops at Gu (Nine) or before, which is smaller than Sip (Ten), it should go back to O (Five) which is the earth and be reborn. Stopping until Gu (Nine) means that a being does not arrive at the finish of Sip (Ten), and Hawn (circulation, 環) means that the chance is reclaimed. On the other hand, if it finishes as Sip (Ten) of InJungCheonJiIl, then it returns to the Mu of the cosmos in accordance with the original purpose. IlJeokSipGeo is the earthly foundation established for this, and the operating way that occurs on top of this foundation is MuGweHwaSam (無櫃化三).

MuGweHwaSam (無櫃化三).
When Gwe is extinct, it becomes Sam (Three).

If IlJeokSipGeo (一積十鉅) is the structural expansion of CheonJiIn, then MuGweHwaSam (無櫃化三) is the structural circulation of CheonJiIn. The standard of the circulation is Gwe (櫃), in other words it is the visible Mu which is the body that contains time. MuGweHwaSam is the way of emergence and extinction of this Gwe (櫃). IlJeok (一積) is the existential separation that is connected with Gwe (櫃) and MuGwe (無櫃), and SipGeo (十鉅) is the base where HwaSam (化三) occurs. MuGwe is about the Byeon (變) which is the disappearance of the visible existential separation, and HwaSam is about Hwa (化) which is the complete transformation of the character. Gwe (櫃) symbolizes 'the state in which all creation has a form'. The box (匱) made with Mu, the material (木) of SeokSamGeuk (析三極), is all creation. Therefore, the Mu of MuGwe (無櫃) means that the box (櫃) returns to Mu. If existence disappears through MuGwe then it returns to its original place through HwaSam. This means that the process where Gwe (櫃) is made with Mu and returns to Mu is repeated in CheonJiIn. This is why GweHwa is the Cheon Bu Gyeong's way of expressing the earthly evolutionary process.

HwaSam (化三) means that the Gwe which is all creation returns to CheonJiIn, that is 1 Un of IlJeokSipGeo (一積十鉅). The reason for returning to the state of CheonJiIn where the cosmos and the Earth are connected is that all creation is created by the cosmic purpose. Through this process, all creation is endowed with new time in 1 Un and born. HwaSam is connected with DaeSamHapYuk (大三合六) and HwanOChil (環五七) and explains that all creation and human are the same beings of Sam (Three). Because all creation returns to

Sam (Three) repeatedly, it can have both the earthly and cosmic properties. HwaSam fills the Mu of 1 Un with the memories and time of Mu contained in the Gwe that had emerged. The Earth uses the time and memories of the Mu added by HwaSam for evolution, and separately apply MuGweHwaSam and HwanOChil according to the evolutionary stages. For this reason all creation and human do not lose their purpose, the cosmic evolution. The Earth that was separated through MuSill (無始一) became self-reliant having SamGeuk as Bon. And through CheonJiIn, it selected human to be the subject for the finish in accordance with the cosmic purpose. MuGweHwaSam is the way of circulation that makes it possible for the Earth which gained self-reliance through SamGeuk to evolve through CheonJiIn.

MuGweHwaSam is the basic principle regarding the circulation of beings within the Earth. This becomes the supply of human through DaeSamHapYuk (大三合六) in 2 Un, and becomes HwanOChil (環五七) that circulates human in 3 Un. All creation and human go back to 1 Un and receive their time until IlJong (一終, finish as One) without exception, and this process is done following the principle of MuGweHwaSam. The only way of escaping this cycle of MuGweHwaSam is the finish. The reason why the Cheon Bu Gyeong does not use the word symbolizing death (死) is that death cannot exist in the cosmos based on Mu. It is only that the Mu contained in a box (櫃) becomes its original Mu after the box disappeared. This process and condition is MuGweHwaSam. The difference between the circulation and the finish depends on whether this Mu of return is the earthly or the cosmic Mu. MuGweHwaSam teaches the existence of Mu by showing the circulation through the stop (死=己).

With the MuGweHwaSam of 1 Un and DaeSam HapYuk of 2 Un, the Cheon Bu Gyeong shows that all creation and human have the equal chances of 3 Un. This is because there is no difference between all creation and human in returning to Sam (Three) through Hwa (化) and receiving time to emerge as human through HapYuk (合六). This means that after the appearance of the evolved human, the chance of the earthly evolution for all creation is still open. The evolution in this case is not the biological evolution but the cosmic evolution. This is why there is no discrimination in returning to Sam (Three) in HwaSam and why HwanOChil which is the circulation of human is connected with HapYuk. The body (櫃) in 3 Un returns to O (五) because it is interlinked with the CheonJiIn of 2 Un in terms of traits, and then it gets scattered to Sam (三) because the time for creating the body is received from 1 Un.

HwaSam (化三) is the process of receiving time interlinked with the cosmos. The time assigned like this is the finite Mu that the being which was born as Gwe has. The Mu that created 'the being which was born' goes back to its original Mu when the box (櫃) that contains it disappears. The Bon of the Earth can maintain the durability of evolution through HwaSam. So the Mu of SamGeuk which has no creation and the Mu of SamJae filled with all creation operate in connection with each other through MuGweHwaSam. This is because the Earth and human cannot escape from the process corresponding to the cosmic purpose. Therefore, UnSam (運三) of human evolution operates in a way that when beings become MuGwe (無櫃) they return to O (五) which is the earth of 2 Un, and then get scattered to Sam (三) of 1 Un through the process of Hwa (化), after that, recombined with Yuk (六) during 3 Un and appear as Chil (七). And this is why the Cheon Bu

Gyeong has sequentially placed MuGwe and HwaSam.

Verse 4

CheonISam, JiISam, InISam (天二三, 地二三, 人二三).

Cheon is Sam (Three), Ji is Sam (Three) and In is Sam (Three) as well in the second operation.

天 Cheon : the sky / 二 I : Two / 三 Sam : Three
地 Ji : the Earth, earth / 二 I : Two / 三 Sam : Three
人 In : human / 二 I : Two / 三 Sam : Three

> **CheonISam, JilSam, InISam (天二三, 地二三, 人二三).**
> Cheon is Sam (Three), Ji is Sam (Three) and In is Sam (Three) as well in the second operation.

This is an explanation regarding 2 Un (2運) which is the second operation of UnSam (運三). If 1 Un (1運) is a process of structuring through the expansion into CheonJiIn (天地人), then 2 Un is a process of integration of CheonJiIn to operate in accordance with the purpose of Bon. The I (Two) of 'CheonISam JiISam InISam (天二三 地二三 人二三)' indicates 2 Un which means the second operation, and Sam (Three) indicates CheonJiIn and all creation of 1 Un (1運). Furthermore, it shows through DaeSamHapYuk (大三合六) that the CheonJi (天地, the sky and the earth) which have become bigger through 2 Un are combined in Sam (三) which is all creation, then become Yuk (Six). 2 Un is the process of structural combination into a state of One through exchange and circulation after the process of 1 Un where each component of CheonJiIn is constructed. The operation corresponding to the evolutionary process becomes possible through the process of 2 Un. Through this all creation becomes compressed into one being for the earthly evolution. This compressed being, human, gets to have the property of expansion due to the directionality of time and the property of combination due to the circularity of time. The fixed base and subject for evolution as well as the principle of operation are completed in 2 Un. After this, change does not occur to the structure and role of CheonJiIn. This is because the flow and the directionality in accordance with the cosmic purpose are stabilized in time and space.

If 1 Un is the process of separation through time, then 2 Un is the process of the earthly integration through space. Each component of CheonJiIn (天地人, The sky, the Earth and human) was established through the flow of time during 1 Un, and during 2 Un the CheonJiIn that has gone through the circulation of time functions in a state of One. It means that Bon which was separated into three during 1 Un is combined again into a state of One. It is a process that the natural flow of CheonJiIn flowing in accordance with SamGeuk (三極) which is Bon and the causality which is the circulation within are operated naturally. Through this process the Earth had continued constantly and was completed as a small cosmos where all creation lives. This is the earthly operating system CheonJiJaYeon (天地自然, the sky, the Earth and nature), and it means that the independent time and space of the Earth becomes matured enough to raise a life. As a result, like SamJae was born and separated from the time and space of SamGeuk, human was separated from the time and space of SamJae.

The Earth becomes independent from the cosmos through IlSiMuSiIl (一始無始一) and then becomes self-reliant through SeokSamGeuk (析三極). And SamGeuk makes human get separated from CheonJiIn and become self-reliant through 1 Un and 2 Un. This is the way of the earthly evolution. The operation of CheonJiIn can continue in one direction because the Earth has gone through the separation and integration process of independence and self-reliance during 1 Un and 2 Un. The straight line of time in 1 Un becomes the circle of time in 2 Un, and in 3 Un the being that was selected gains the directionality of evolution composed of both straight line and circle. This process changes the main agent of operation. This is the reason why the main agent continues to be changed. SamGeuk is the main agent of 1 Un, CheonJiIn is that of 2 Un and human is that of 3 Un. 'One begins, the One becomes Three and the Three becomes One again and then finish as Mu.'

This is the operating principle of the Cheon Bu Gyeong. In this process, human becomes the only being on the Earth that can finish as Mu. 2 Un created the everlasting time and space where the earthly evolution continues and emerges. Through this the space that holds time was established as the time and space for the earthly evolution. For this reason, the body symbolizing the spatial result as well as circulation in HwanOChil (環五七) returns to 2 Un, and is endowed with time in 1 Un and then comes back.

The Earth divided through SeokSamGeuk (析三極) completes CheonJiIn with the integrated time and space during 2 Un. In 2 Un CheonJiIn becomes the base interlinked with one another as one for the first time. To the CheonJiIn formed in this way, the numbers of Sa (Four), O (Five) and Yuk (Six) are assigned according to the order of 1 Un (CheonIl, JiI and InSam) and the circulation of 2 Un. InISam (人二三) of 2 Un symbolizes human. Through this process all creation gains its evolutionary meaning, and human becomes established as the main agent of evolution among all creation. The basis for this can be found in DaeSamHapYuk (大三合六). It symbolizes that CheonJi is combined into all creation which is Sam (three) of 2 Un. This principle applies to BonSim (本心) and InJungCheonJiIl (人中天地一) in the same way.

The reason that 2 Un is 'CheonISam JiISam InISam (天二三 地二三 人二三)' rather than 'CheonISa JiIO InIYuk (天二四 地二五 人二六)' according to the sequential order of 1 Un should be examined. This is because 1 Un is the process in which CheonJiIn is born from SamGeuk, and 2 Un is the combination process of the existing CheonJiIn. This shows the differences in process between being born and structuralization of what has been born. The main agent of this integration is Sam (三) of SamJae, and the subject of this integration is Sam (三) which is all creation of the InIlSam (人一三). Therefore, 2 Un is written as 'CheonISam JiISam InISam' unlike the sequential order of 1 Un, which shows that each of CheonJiIn gets to have the property of SamGeuk which is Bon. Furthermore, it shows that CheonJi (天地, the sky and the Earth), which are Il (One) and I (Two) each, raise and are combined into Sam (Three), all creation existing in the space between them. It is because the Earth is born for the cosmic purpose of evolution, and the subject of that evolution is all creation (三) rather than CheonJi (天地). Therefore, Sam (Three) is expanded and combined through 'CheonISam JiISam InISam' and then becomes Yuk (Six) as a base. And the Yuk as a base raises and combines all creation, Sam (Three) to carry out the existential evolution into human who is Yuk (Six) as a being.

Verse 5

DaeSamHapYuk (大三合六),

Sam (Three) is expanded and combined into Yuk (Six)

SaengChilPalGu (生七八九).

To be born as Chil (Seven), Pal (Eight) and Gu (Nine).

大 Dae : expand, raise / 三 Sam : Three / 合 Hap : combine / 六 Yuk : Six
生 Saeng : live / 七 Chil : Seven / 八 Pal : Eight / 九 Gu : Nine

DaeSamHapYuk (大三合六),
Sam (Three) is expanded and combined into Yuk (Six)

Sam (Three) of DaeSam indicates CheonJiIn, the base and all creation, the subject. Dae (大) means expansion of CheonJiIn and raising all creation. HapYuk (合六) is the result of that. It symbolizes the expanded and combined state of CheonJiIn and human as the being which is the combination of raised all creation. DaeSam (大三) is that SamGeuk is expanded into CheonJiIn with one purpose through the process of 1 Un and 2 Un. Each component of CheonJiIn SamJae keeps the other two components and is expanded to Sam (Three). Expansion means that Cheon (the sky), Ji (the Earth) and In (human) are overlapped as a complete state of One, and means that the Earth operates according to one purpose. This one purpose is the existential evolution in accordance with the cosmic evolutionary process. DaeSamHapYuk (大三合六) means that the base of CheonJiIn becomes bigger and combined for this purpose, and also means that it raises and combines the subject of evolution. Therefore, DaeSam (大三), connected with HapYuk (合六), explains the existential evolution and indicates that its subject is all creation of Sam (Three) which is the only being of evolution among CheonJiIn. All creation becomes expanded and combined with holding CheonJi and then becomes evolutionally independent. Through this process, all creation becomes Yuk (Six). Also, DaeSamHapYuk (大三合六) of 2 Un shows that CheonJiIn will repeat to combine all creation into the being of Yuk (六).

SamGeuk made CheonJiIn through time for evolution. UnSam (運三) is the process that explains this. 1 Un and IlJeokSipGeo (一積十鉅) show the accumulation which is the straight characteristic of time. 2 Un and DaeSamHapYuk (大三合六) show the expansion (大) and combination (合) which are the circulatory characteristic of time. In SaengChilPalGu (生七八九) of 3 Un which is the result of them, the existential evolution of human is operated under the combined effects of directionality and circularity of time. This is the reason that the separated CheonJiIn of 1 Un becomes expanded and combined into Yuk (Six) in 2 Un. The number of 1 Un where CheonJiIn is created is Sam (Three), and the number of 2 Un where CheonJiIn is combined becomes Yuk (Six). According to this, the symbolic number of SamGeuk which created CheonJiIn becomes Sam (Three) and that of the completed CheonJiIn SamJae becomes Yuk (Six). On this principle, Yuk (Six) is the evolutionary result of Sam (Three) which is all creation, and Gu (Nine) is the evolutionary result of human which is Yuk (Six). This is because the Earth is created for the evolution into the being in accordance with the cosmic purpose, and Yuk (Six) which is the result of expansion and combination of all creation, Sam (Three), symbolizes human. Therefore it can be known that human is born as the being of HapYuk on top of CheonJiIn which is HapYuk. During 2 Un, SamGeuk made Sam (Three) of CheonJiIn into Yuk (Six) in a state of one, and CheonJiIn selected human among all creation which is Sam (Three) as the representative of evolution which is Yuk (Six).

According to the order of CheonIl JiI InSam in 1 Un, Cheon becomes Sa (Four), Ji becomes O (Five), and In becomes Yuk (Six) in 2 Un. SamGeuk which is Bon selected human to be the only evolutionary subject among all creation through DaeSamHapYuk (大三合六). This is the reason why human, not like all creation, can combine CheonJi (天地) inside himself. The base of this combination is a place for the Mind made through HapYuk (合六), and the state of combination in process is

BonSim (本心), and the combination through the finish is InJungCheonJiIl (人中天地一). HapYuk (合六) is the state that the base and subject for the finish is ready as Yuk (Six) on the Earth, therefore, CheonJiIn which is Yuk (Six) operates in a state of one for the finish. In this process, if human who is Yuk (Six) goes through IlMyoYeon (一妙衍) and completes the combination of CheonJiIn, then he becomes Gu (Nine) who has the Mind (心). By following the principle by which human is created through DaeSamHapYuk, BonSim is made through DaeYukHapGu (大六合九) where human goes through SamByeon (三變).

CheonJiIn came to share one purpose through DaeSamHapYuk (大三合六). Cheon (the sky) which is Il (One) and Ji (the earth) which is I (Two) become expanded and then combined inside all creation which is Sam (Three). And the combination becomes Yuk (Six). Through DaeSamHapYuk, preparing both Yuk (Six) as the base for the evolution in accordance with the purpose of the cosmos and Yuk (Six) as its subject has completed. This means that Sam (Three) becomes expanded and then combined into Yuk (Six). All creation which had been an individual being during 1 Un, held CheonJi and made human independent in 2 Un. And Gu (Nine) is that the independent human becomes self-reliant through this kind of way. In this way, the Cheon Bu Gyeong evolutionarily separates human which is Yuk (Six) from all creation which is Sam (Three). Therefore, the Cheon Bu Gyeong explains that the earthly evolution in accordance with the cosmic purpose is a process that the expanded and divided through IlJeokSipGeo returns to Bon with the repetition of being combined. And this is the reason that the Cheon Bu Gyeong places Yuk (Six) which is the being as well as the base that symbolizes expansion and combination in the center of the eighty-one letters.

The existential evolution of Sam (Three) into Yuk (Six) and Yuk (Six) into Gu (Nine) again is the process of the earthly evolution in accordance with the cosmic purpose. And this is the reason why the Earth goes through the process of creating CheonJiManMul (the sky, the earth and all creation, 天地萬物) through IlJeokSipGeo (一積十鉅) and selecting human among all creation through DaeSamHapYuk (大三合六). Therefore, if Sam (Three) is all creation including human before he was selected as the subject of evolution, then Yuk (Six) is the symbol of human that has gone through the process of GweHwa (櫃化) to have a place for the Mind which is Bon. However, Yuk (Six) which has become expanded and combined, is placed in a state where all creation has a chance to challenge to finish. This is the difference in meaning between human of HapYuk (合六) and human of SaengChil (生七). Only human who has gone through SaengChil (生七) can use CheonJi (天地) for evolution. After HapYuk (合六), only the journey to Sip (Ten) remains. The Cheon Bu Gyeong says that all creation has been combined into Yuk (Six) which is the number symbolizing human, and when it is born as a human symbolized with SaengChil (生七) it can get the opportunity. In this way, human and all creation who share the state of Yuk (Six) are not different. All creation is like a mother in the evolutionary process of human, and if human cannot get BuDongBon (不動本) then he has to go back to all creation.

SaengChilPalGu (生七八九).
To be born as Chil (Seven), Pal (Eight) and Gu (Nine).

SaengChilPalGu (生七八九) is 3 Un which is the final operation of UnSam (運三). 3 Un is the process where both the base of the earthly evolution and the subject of human, as a state of one, challenge the finish to correspond to the cosmic purpose. Chil (Seven), Pal (Eight) and Gu (Nine) symbolize the existential evolutionary process of human who has been born, and their standards can be examined by the connection with the procedural characteristics of IlMyoYeon (一妙衍). CheonJiIn was completed through the process of 2 Un, and the base of the evolution as well as the operating way of its subject was decided. SaengChilPalGu is a process of living life as a human, and indicates the repetition of life's circulation. In other words, it is the evolutionary process of human challenging the finish on top of CheonJiIn of 2 Un. Therefore, SaengChilPalGu is the final evolutionary process where all creation is operated as human in the Cheon Bu Gyeong. It is the process where the process of DaeSamHapYuk (大三合六) that occurred in CheonJiIn which is Sam (Three) happens in human which is Yuk (Six). SaengChilPalGu means that human should follow the natural flow of the Earth and go through the process of Chil (Seven) and Pal (Eight) to expand up to Gu (Nine). This is because human is the only evolutionary being which was born from the combined Yuk (Six), and because Gu (Nine) is the biggest number human can reach within the Earth which is Sip (Ten).

The process of InJungCheonJiIl (人中天地一) which is Sip (Ten) during the process of IlMyoYeon (一妙衍) is not the process of the earthly evolution, but the cosmic evolution. All of Chil (Seven), Pal (Eight) and Gu (Nine) can be connected during one single life, or each metempsychosis steps of SaengChil (生七) • SaengPal (生八) • SaengGu (生九) should be taken step by step. All creation comes from SamGeuk, so it cannot be bigger than Sip (Ten) of SipGeo (十鉅). The purpose of evolution is overcoming the limit, and the only being that can do this is human. To arrive at Sip (Ten) and finish as Mu is to cross the earthly border of Sip (Ten) and becomes a state of the cosmic Mu. If SaengChilPalGu (生七八九) of human does not finish as Sip (Ten), then it must go back to the loop of circulation. The meaning of Chil (Seven), Pal (Eight) and Gu (Nine) is that the procedural fruit during the loop of circulation can make a difference in the opportunity of being born. In this process, Chil (Seven) is just a being that is operated by the time of the sky. If it goes through the process and place its root on the earth, then it becomes Pal (八) and is able to circulate as human. And if it realizes Bon existentially, then it becomes Gu (Nine) that has the Mind and circulates as the Self (我).

The Cheon Bu Gyeong tries to teach one principle that is applied equally to the cosmos and the Earth as well as all creation and human. It is the basic rule of survival and evolution that is applied throughout all creation, and it explains the reason that all creation and human should evolve without stopping. For this, the Earth goes through the process of evolving the base and the subject sequentially. And there is an evolutionary separation of Chil (Seven), Pal (Eight) and Gu (Nine) in human as well. In this way, SaengChilPalGu shows that the evolutionary steps of Chil (Seven), Pal (Eight) and Gu (Nine) must be taken by using life for evolution. While taking these steps, Chil (Seven) uses instinct of all creation, Pal (Eight) uses human emotion, and Gu (Nine) uses the Mind of the Self (我). And it is the evolution of IlMyoYeon (一妙衍).

A being that is born from what already began cannot escape from the continuation of life whose right and responsibility is the finish.

From the position of IlSi (一始), SaengChilPalGu (生七八九) is being born separated from the process of 1Un and 2 Un. If HapYuk is creating a being in accordance with the position of IlSi (一始), then SaengChilPalGu is that the being becomes in accordance with the purpose of evolution with life. Chil (Seven) is the stage where human of HapYuk is placed in the first step of evolution as human. This can also be known through HwanOChil (環五七). Because Chil (Seven) circulates in the place of all creation, it shares the state of Yuk (Six). Therefore, being born as human again is not guaranteed. Through the repetition of these processes, human passes the process of Chil (Seven) and evolves into Pal (Eight) and Gu (Nine) to be born little by little closer to a state of Sip (Ten). For this reason, SaengChilPalGu (生七八九) is the UnSam of human existential evolutionary process. It is easier for human to arrive at Sip (Ten) when he was born in a state of Gu (Nine). So Chil (Seven), Pal (Eight) and Gu (nine) which are used as the different evolutionary stages of human reveal the natural capability differences of human. This evolutionary journey of SaengChilPalGu (生七八九) can be explained according to the characteristics of human existential states. Chil (Seven) is human as all creation, Pal (Eight) is human as human, Gu (Nine) is human as a saint (聖人), and InJungCheonJiIl (人中天地一) which is Sip (Ten) becomes human as God.

Human, different from all creation, circulates in the separate way called HwanOChil (環五七). This is because the being of human should be repeated evolutionarily. If the place where it is decided to be born is all creation then it is Chil (Seven), if human then Pal (Eight), and if the Self (我) then Gu (Nine). Therefore, SaengChilPalGu (生七八九) connected to HwanOChil suggests that human must escape from HwanOChil (環五七) into HwanOPal (環五八) or HwanOGu (環五九). ChilPalGu (Seven, Eight and Nine) is that human experiences the process of Sam (Three) becoming Yuk (Six) inside himself. Therefore, if born as human, abandoning the competitive instinct of all creation and living a life of evolution as human is needed. Yuk (Six) is the field where the grass expands thick with no separation, Chil (Seven) is getting rid of the grass to make a place for foundation, and Pal (Eight) is like building a house on top of that foundation. And

Gu (Nine) is a process of finishing the completed house by decorating with the Mind. This is the process of human building a house which will contain CheonJi (天地) that is the Mind (心) through HapYuk (合六) and SaengChilPalGu. In order to be born in a state close to Sip (Ten), human must evolve by regarding Saeng (生) and Hwan (環) not as a purpose, but as an opportunity. This is the process of human making BonSim (本心), and it is the unchanging character of the Mind. Therefore, all the religions which serve Gods (humans who arrive at the finish) tell about the Mind. Buddha called this 'the nature of Buddha (佛性)', Jesus called it 'God within you', and Lao Tzu called it 'Do (道)'.

Verse 6

UnSam (運三),

The principle of operation is Sam (Three)

SaSeong (四成),

The principle of completion is Sa (Four)

HwanOChil (環五七).

The principle of circulation is O (Five) and Chil (Seven).

運 Un : operate / 三 Sam : Three
四 Sa : Four / 成 Seong : complete
環 Hwan : circulate, repeat / 五 O : Five / 七 Chil : Seven

UnSam (運三),
The principle of operation is Sam (Three)

UnSam (運三) means 'both the Sam (Three) which operates and the three times of operations (三運)'. Un (運) is the continuing flow of time, and Sam (Three) is its subject. Sam (Three) is CheonJiIn in the perspective of the earthly evolution, and all creation in the perspective of the existential evolution. And when these two types of Sam (Three) are in operation, it indicates the three stages. In this phased process, it is UnSam that the Sam of CheonJiIn SamJae which is the base of evolution and the Sam of all creation which is the subject of evolution operate in a state of one. In the Cheon Bu Gyeong each stages of UnSam is tied with the result of the operation. The structure of 1Un is that three components of CheonJiIn begin and become expanded through IlJeokSipGeo and circulate through MuGweHwaSam. In 2 Un, the expanded CheonJiIn circulates as a state of one and raises and combines all creation into human who is the representative and the being of evolution. 3 Un is a process of human going through the path of One in accordance with the cosmic purpose on top of CheonJiIn of HapYuk through SaengChilPalGu.

The reason the Cheon Bu Gyeong uses UnSam (運 三) rather than SamUn (三運) is to show a difference in meaning from the SaSeong (四成) which appears subsequently. If UnSam is the process where the earthly subjects, time and space operate, then SaSeong (四成) means the four times of processes including UnSam and the fruit born in the fourth process. This is because even though three operations and completion in the fourth process are connected, they function independently of each other. SaSeong ties a knot to the repeated process of UnSam, and this is the principle that creates difference and repetition in the evolutionary process. It is through the process of changing the base and subject during UnSam that the evolutionary completion of SaSeong is repeated. The evolutionary being is operated three times as Sam (Three), Yuk (Six) and Gu (Nine) on the base of CheonJiIn. This is a process of preparing time and space of the Earth to be suitable for the cosmic purpose, and is the evolving process of this evolutionary subject by keeping the earthly time and space one by one.

UnSam begins in the first operation with the creation of CheonJi (天地) and all creation which have the time of SamGeuk. In the second operation, CheonJi and all creation become one to form an organic structure of DaeSam (大三), and then select human as an evolutionary subject through HapYuk (合六). In the third operation, an evolutionary process of SaengChilPalGu (生七八九) that is applied only to human occurs. In other words, UnSam is completing the earthly evolutionary system that operates both human and ChoenIi (天地) which were created on the Earth as a state of one. UnSam is the process of establishing one single principle and subject from the complex and overlapped structures as well as its subject on top. As a result, human goes through IlMyoYeon (一妙衍) with SaengChilPalGu which is the existential UnSam and arrives at SaSeong (四成) with InJungCheonJiIl (人中天地一). SaSeong of human in CheonJiIn which is in a state of HapYuk (合六) is BonSim (本心) of Gu (Nine), and SaSeong of human in SamGeuk is the cosmic finish. This is the reason why SaSeong and HwanOChil (環五七) where the finish or the circulation is determined occurs after UnSam.

UnSam is thrice changing process of the earthly SamByeon (三變). UnSam occurs within Sip (Ten) which is the number of the Earth. Human circulates or finishes according to the result of operation. Because all creation is connected through the process of UnSam, it is given the opportunity as human to challenge the finish. In this way, UnSam is a process that gives all creation the chance to be the subject of the cosmic evolution as the Earth has the separate time and space from the cosmos. Human who is the only existential symbol of this chance also goes through the UnSam process as Chil (Seven), Pal (Eight) and Gu (Nine). During this process there is no existential hierarchy or a fixed order between all creation and human. And there is no priority in arriving at the finish either. This means that even if a being became a human earlier, it could arrive at the finish later. Therefore, Sip (Ten) which is the border between the earthly evolution and the cosmic evolution is SaSeong which is the goal of UnSam.

In the process of UnSam, the order and numbers from Il (One) to Gu (Nine) are decided. The basis of assigning the numbers is the order of being born in 1 Un, and the number is assigned to CheonJiIn. This is because the only sequential arrangement in the Cheon Bu Gyeong is CheonIlIl JiIlI InIlSam (天一一地一二人一三) of 1 Un. After that, all the changes and evolutions occur within the CheonJiIn. For this reason, the numbers of 1, 4 and 7 are assigned to Cheon (the sky), 2, 5 and 8 are assigned to Ji (the earth), and 3, 6 and 9 are assigned to In (human). Through this it can be confirmed that DaeSam (大三), HapYuk (合六), and SaengChilPalGu (生七八九) are the numbers whose purpose is In (human). Through this order, the meaning behind the three processes of UnSam can be examined. During 1 Un, CheonJiIn is born and has the time which is the property of Cheon (the sky). During 2 Un, CheonJiIn becomes the base which is the property of Ji (earth) circulating interlinked one another. During 3 Un, CheonJiIn evolves the being with the time and base, and becomes the Mind which is the property of human (人). Through the loops of these circulations, Sip (Ten) which is the state of InJungCheonJiIl (人中天地一) can be reached. Through the operations of UnSam, the Cheon Bu Gyeong clearly shows that 1 Un is a process for Sam (Three) which is all creation, 2 Un is for Yuk (Six) which is human, and 3 Un is for Gu (Nine) which has Bon.

SaSeong (四成),
The principle of completion is Sa (Four)

SaSeong (四成) is about the knot which is the result following the operation of UnSam. Sa (Four) indicates the process of what was happened by UnSam being completed, and Seong (成) indicates the result. In other words, SaSeong is combining each result from the operation processes of UnSam. If compared to four seasons, it means that the Seong (成) of spring, the Seong (成) of summer, and the Seong (成) of autumn are all combined to determine SaSeong (四成) which is the Seong (成) of winter. For this reason it is UnSam and SaSeong. According to this result, life of human circulates with HwanOChil (環五七) or ends with the finish. The SaSeong of the Cheon Bu Gyeong makes it as a goal to do SaSeong as the cosmic Mu by going through UnSam of the earthly Mu. Therefore, the Mu of MuGwe which is the stop of life and the Mu of MuJongIl which arrives at the finish are different. This is because the being born (生) and the beginning (始) of the being are decided through this.

SaSeong (四成) is similar to the principle of four seasons

of the Earth which circulate with being connected one another. If spring, summer and autumn are UnSam then winter which is the result is SaSeong. Spring, summer and autumn, each season operates according to its own characteristics, and one loop of circulation (spring-summer-autumn-winter) is completed through winter. For this reason, winter is a time of pause rather than change unlike the other seasons. Four seasons of the Earth are separated and operated under the influence of the sun. This is the reason why the Mind, human Bon made in the process, follows the sun. As human resembles this process by being born and stopping, the existential evolution continues. For this, there are two ways in SaSeong. One is the finish which is the evolutionary purpose, and the other is HwanOChil (環五七) which is repeated challenges to the finish. In other words, if UnSam achieves the finish, then it continues in the finished state rather than going back to circulation. If a human truly loves the current Self (我), then he must try to finish and continue in the state of the present Self (我). This is the only way where a human can make the given life valuable. HwanOChil comes after SaSeong in order to show that this process continues until it is completed.

The circulation of SaSeong (四成) shows that the evolution for human to arrive at the finish is not a choice, but an absolute obligation. SaSeong is the process of completion, and is basically composed of 4 stages. For the cosmos, the completion should be examined in 4 stages too. The process of SaSeong is composed of 4 stages. The Earth, what had begun as One is stage 1. It is divided into three during SeokSamGeuk (析三極), stage 2. CheonJiIn, stage 3 combines them again into a state of One. And then human, the evolutionary being completes the evolution in stage 4. For the Earth, the process of SaSeong is as follows. Bon which is SamGeuk creates CheonJiIn. The CheonJiIn creates human. The human goes through the existential evolutionary process through UnSam. And then he finishes with InJungCheonJiIl. The life of human also follows the process of UnSam and SaSeong. This is the principle in the Cheon Bu Gyeong that human goes through SaengChilPalGu (生七八九) and arrives at InJungCheonJiIl (人中天地一). It explains UnSam of human from stage 1 to 3 with SaengChilPalGu and explains stage 4 with InJungCheonJiIl.

The Mind is the result from the selective evolution of

the Earth as well as its proof, and only human can make and have it. It is because the Mind was made in human that human can finish by containing CheonJi. The Cheon Bu Gyeong says that having the Mind of human is also SaSeong, and indicates with BonSim (本心) that it could be gained through the circulation process of Yuk (Six), Chil (Seven) and Pal (Eight). For this human escapes from human of all creation which is HapYuk (合六) into SaengChil (生七). One which has begun or been born generally goes through the process of 4 stages like this. Therefore, SaSeong is decided according to the results of the operation process of UnSam. This means that a result different from the process does not occur, and this is the reason that the result and the beginning can be linked together. The Cheon Bu Gyeong says this process in two forms. The first is the stage of overall completion that the change processes from 1 Un to 3 Un and the result of the finish are combined. The continuous form of circulation from 1 to 9 and the complete finish are included here. And the second is regarding the partial completion that what has begun as One continues as life. This is completing one life within the loop of circulation composed of being divided, being expanded, being combined and stopping.

HwanOChil (環五七).
The principle of circulation is O (Five) and Chil (Seven).

HwanOChil (環五七) is about the circulation due to the stop (死, death) among SaSeong (四成). It is applied to SaengChilPalGu of human and means that the opportunity of life is repeated. Human can repeat his evolution through life thanks to the circulation process of HwanOChil. The Cheon Bu Gyeong clearly separates the existence of human from that of all creation by circulating as Chil (七). Most of humans go through MuGweHwaSam by stopping instead of arriving at the finish. Also, most of humans are placed between the stages of Yuk (Six) and Chil (Seven). This is because they cannot escape to be independent from the survival which is the instinct of all creation on the path of evolution. It is the reason why they cannot accept the path of the finish shown by Buddha, Jesus and Lao Tzu. The competition of human makes them not realize that human is in the process of connecting life and life to have the Mind as an individual independent being. For this reason, it is not easy to escape the loop of HwanOChil and go over to Pal (Eight). Therefore, we must not misuse the chance given by HwanOChil being placed after SaSeong.

HwanOChil is the process of circulation that is repeated within CheonJiIn, and acts as a restraint that cannot be undone without the will towards BuDongBon (不動本) as human.

There should be a stop to what has been born, so being reborn to arrive at the finish is the natural process. However, the evolution of human does not occur naturally. This is the reason why human follows nature to resemble it. HwanOChil (環五七) is a loop of returning to Ji of CheonJiIn to receive new time and then being reborn. This is because the number of the earth in CheonJiIn of 2 Un where SaengChilPalGu of 3 Un is operated is O (Five), and because human is operated on the base made in 2 Un. And Chil (Seven) symbolizes that human of HapYuk (合六) receives a new time for life in 1 Un (1運). In this way, three operations of UnSam continue in a state of one. Therefore, Chil (seven) is the number symbolizing the sky which is time according to the classification of CheonJiIn and symbolizing new human according to the evolutionary classification. Thereby continues to receive the opportunity to challenge the process of Pal (Eight) and Gu (Nine) to arrive at Sip (Ten). This occurs equally to all creation.

HwanOChil (環五七) is the same as being replicated (母) in the Do Deok Gyeong (道德經, Tao Te Ching in Chinese), and SaengChil (生七) is the act of human 'putting down roots on CheonJi (天地根)'.

The beginning of the subject that flows through IlMyoYeon (一妙衍) in the Cheon Bu Gyeong is Chil (Seven). In HwanOChil (環五七) for this, UnSam and SaSeong have different meanings. UnSam has the role of the sky to revive what has stopped to operate constantly. For this reason UnSam which is the flow of time is the property of the sky in the Cheon Bu Gyeong. On the other hand, SaSeong (四成) is revealing the fruit from the completion of what has been born. And the result of completion is revealed on the Earth. So SaSeong is the property of the Earth (地). The time of the sky relies on the property of the earth when Chil (Seven), what has been born transfers to Pal (Eight). Pal (Eight) is different from Chil (Seven) which receives time from the sky in that it gained the qualification to circulate as human. For this reason, human in a state of Chil (Seven) looks up to the sky, human in a state of Pal (Eight) tries to follow nature with his given time, and human in a state of Gu (Nine) follows the Mind which is his own Bon as well as Mu in order to correspond to the cosmos. The evolutionary way of circulation continues with connecting all creation with human through HwanOChil, connecting human with human through HwanOPal (環五八), and connecting human with the Self (我) through HwanOGu (環五九). This is the image of metempsychosis (輪廻), and the circulation of HwanOGu (環五九) among these is the true metempsychosis.

The circulation of HwanOChil explains repetition by HwanO (環五) and HwanChil (環七). HwanO (環五) is the stop which means what has been born returns, and HwanChil (環七) is being reborn. Combination of UnSam of CheonJiIn and the results of each stage also becomes Chil (Seven). In this way, Chil (Seven) is the life of human as an identical evolutionary being. Therefore, Hwan (環) is a tool of operation in order to go forward in the evolutionary direction of Pal (Eight) and Gu (Nine) through circulation. Chil (Seven), Pal (Eight) and Gu (Nine) are the symbols of the earthly beings that must experience the circulation process again. HwanOChil that connects Yuk (Six) and Chil (Seven) in the Cheon Bu Gyeong carries an important distinction. Human starting from Pal (Eight) does not return to all creation. It means that he is placed in the stage where life as human is repeated. This is explained through the characteristics of IlMyoYeon (一妙衍) which are ManWangManRae (萬往萬來) and YongByeonBuDongBon (用變不動本). Compared to nature, Chil (Seven) is an annual grass, Pal (Eight) is a flower-bearing perennial, and Gu (Nine) is a gigantic tree that can bear fruit to raise new trees.

The evolution of Chil (Seven), Pal (Eight) and Gu (Nine) is determined according to the existence or nonexistence of the Mind, its size, and how constantly it continues without change. For this reason, until DaeSamHapYuk, the Cheon Bu Gyeong is about the base and subject of evolution. And UnSam (運三), SaSeong (四成) and HwanOChil (環五七) is about the principle of operation. On the contrary, starting from IlMyoYeon, it explains the evolutionary way and standard that the base and subject flows through Un (運), Seong (成) and Hwan (環). Therefore, the explanation connecting the process of IlMyoYeon and SaengChilPalGu is possible. ManWangManRae (萬往萬來) is a process and standard of indistinguishable Chil (Seven), YongByeonBuDongBon (用變不動本) is a process and standard of Pal (Eight) whose Bon as human does not change, and BonSim (本心) is a process and standard of Gu (Nine) who has the Mind as Bon and does BonTaeYangAngMyeong (本太陽昂明). For this reason, Chil (Seven) that does not have the existential Bon of BuDongBon (不動本) and the earthly Bon of BonSim cannot escape from the circulation loop of all creation. In the Cheon Bu Gyeong, the stop and the finish are clearly distinguished and used in separate ways. UnSam, SaSeong, and HwanOChil are used as connecting links between the stop and the finish in the flow of evolution.

Verse 7

IlMyoYeon (一妙衍),
The flow of Il (One) is mysterious

ManWangManRae (萬往萬來),
Even though it comes and goes ten thousand times

YongByeonBuDongBon (用變不動本).
Usage changes but Bon does not move.

一 Il：One / 妙 Myo：mysterious / 衍 Yeon：flow
萬 Man：Ten thousand / 往 Wang：go / 萬 Man：Ten thousand / 來 Rae：come
用 Yong：use, usage / 變 Byeon：change / 不 Bu：not / 動 Dong：move / 本 Bon：the Root

IlMyoYeon (一妙衍),
The flow of Il (One) is mysterious

Il (One) of IlMyoYeon (一妙衍) is the cosmos, the Earth, and all creation, and the flow (衍) is being connected endlessly, and the mystery (妙) is the image that it continues naturally and constantly. IlMyoYeon (一妙衍) is the continuation of evolution process, and its flow never stops. The stop of what has begun is the death of the Earth, and the stop of One's flowing indicates the extinction of human and all creation. For this reason, the flow of One continues constantly. Nevertheless, there are no changes or discrepancy in following the earthly Bon. IlMyoYeon in the Cheon Bu Gyeong is the entirety of the earthly evolutionary process and symbolizes the evolutionary process of independent human. The Cheon Bu Gyeong shows that the process of SaengChilPalGu (生七八九) can be explained with IlMyoYeon by placing IlMyoYeon after being born (生) of human as well as UnSam (運三), SaSeong (四成) and HwanOChil (環五七). For this reason, ManWangManRae (萬往萬來), YongByeonBuDongBon (用變不動本) and BonSim (本心) which are the process of IlMyoYean become the classification and the standard of the process. ManWangManRae continues throughout the entire process until the finish of human, YongByeonBuDongBon operates only in Pal (Eight) and Gu (Nine), and BonSim (本心) only operates in Gu (Nine). Through this the phased characteristic of ChilPalGu (七八九) and the way of moving onto the next step can be known.

If human stops during the process of IlMyoYeon, he returns. Saeng (生, Being born) and Hwan (環, Circulation) flows undoubtedly according to the evolutionary stage of ChilPalGu (七八九). This is expressed as mysterious because it is beyond the understanding of human. It is mysterious that human, the subject of the flow, continues to be suitable for each evolutionary stage. And the principle is also mysterious that the process of evolution constantly flows, which makes the subject step the stages of evolution. Because this mystery keeps delicacy, it is hard to clearly understand even if it is seen. Human is in the circulation loop of IlMyoYeon as a state of One. And he is able to evolve because he is the main agent of the flow. If human evolves into the cosmic being like the Earth as a result of this flow, then he can clearly understand the principle of IlMyoYeon and the image of the flow. Human who has become this type of being is called MuJongIl (無終一) or God.

One is a starting point begun through IlSiMuSiIl (一始無始一). Generally it is the Earth itself, and specifically it means each of all creation created within. The original IlMyoYeon (一妙衍) is the operating way and standard of the Earth itself. Therefore, it is also IlMyoYeon that the single representative of the Earth flows to correspond to the purpose of the cosmos. Because all the beings within the Earth share the same Bon and operating way, they can evolve in one direction in the way suitable for each stage. Flowing in a state of One like this indicates that the life of beings and Bon which operates it are interlinked through one principle. And this is the reason that the flow can be consistent without any discrepancy. Nevertheless, it is difficult for human to clearly understand it until he goes through InJungCheonJiIl (人中天地一) and becomes equal to the Earth. This is because human cannot stay at any single point of Saeng (生) or Hwan (環), and it is only when he has gone through the entire process that the start and the end of the flow can be seen.

The Cheon Bu Gyeong clearly states through

IlMyoYeon (一妙衍) that human is the One that cannot be replaced with any other being. One which was begun or born repeats evolution through the process of Un (運), Seong (成), Hwan (環), and continues to flow in accordance with each stage until it reaches the finish (終). There may be the stop of individual being within IlMyoYeon (一妙衍), but the evolution of One which was begun never stops. This process is fair, impartial, definite, and continues constantly. Because the Earth is operating human in accordance with the purpose of the cosmos which is the finish, human cannot escape from this flow. The only way of escape is to arrive at the finish. The flow of One is the image of the Earth itself, and the mystery is explained by nature which absolutely occurs, even though its flow is extremely complex. And human must exactly follow that in order to have the Mind.

The One of the Cheon Bu Gyeong means the existential Earth which is the cosmic being, and means again the earthly beings, all creation. In IlMyoYeon (一妙衍) process of the evolutionary being, human becomes the One. And it is Bon that connects and interlinks the higher and lower One. Therefore, it flows from

ManWangManRae (萬往萬來) state where the existential Bon is absent to BuDongBon (不動本) which has Bon of human. And IlMyoYeon is the process of concentration where human of BuDongBon has BonSim (本心) as the Self of an independent One. The Earth is a replica (母) of the cosmos for a purpose, and human is what was replicated again for the purpose, so there is no escape from the cosmic principle of change and evolution. Only the result seems different according to the change in use. Human was selected for evolution, but there is no consideration for human until he arrives at BonSim (本心). In the same way, the Earth and human can exist only when it is in accordance with the purpose of the cosmos.

ManWangManRae (萬往萬來),
Even though it comes and goes ten thousand times

ManWangManRae (萬往萬來) is the process of circulation where IlMyoYeon (一妙衍) is connected through time. Therefore, it can be understood with the connection of Chil (Seven) which is the being created by time in the evolutionary process of SaengChilPalGu (生七八九). In other words, this means that it only comes and goes with time, but cannot make any changes. Even if the being was born as human, he does not have BuDongBon (不動本) as human. Additionally, ManWangManRae is a flow characteristic of MuGweHwaSam (無櫃化三) that continues circulating until it arrives at the finish. If the being escapes from natural instinct of all creation and has Bon as human in the process of ManWangManRae, then it can be Pal (Eight). The stop of life and the finish of the beginning are possible because of ManWangManRae.

ManWangManRae is overflowing without separation. Only the being that has Bon can go through ManWangManRae in which only the usage changes with Bon. And that is why YongByeonBuDongBon (用變不動本) comes after ManWangManRae. The Earth is not concerned with the existential life that goes through ManWangManRae. The Earth evolves it into Chil (Seven), Pal (Eight) and Gu (Nine) according to the result of its life and only maintains the stage. This is because the Earth exists for the cosmic evolution. If a being has BonSim (本心) which is the qualification to correspond to the purpose of the cosmos, then it can go through ManWangManRae as the Self in a state of One. There are two different aspects in ManWangManRae. First is the ManWangManRae of the earthly aspect that various creations continue to come and go. Second is the ManWangManRae of human aspect that human repeats life until arrives at the finish. Human repeats being born and going back like a loop in the time and space of CheonJiIn.

ManWangManRae (萬往萬來) shows that time goes by without a break and beings are repeated in IlMyoYeon (一妙衍). ManWangManRae is a circulation, and this is because the IlMyoYeon of the Earth flows on top of 2 Un. SamGeuk which is Bon continues to give the opportunity for the finish through ManWangManRae in order to maintain CheonJiIn which is the time and space for this until achieves the purpose. Creating and destroying stars of the cosmos is the way of the cosmic ManWangManRae, and the Earth also follows this way. The Earth continues to make human go through ManWangManRae in the cosmos, and other stars also go through ManWangManRae in order to correspond to the purpose given by the cosmos. Through this process, the stars in accordance with the purpose of evolution are created in the cosmos, and again the star where the evolution actually occurs like the Earth is created among them. ManWangManRae is that this process is applied to human. So, human must become YongByeonBuDongBon (用變不動本) to evolve into a complete human, and then he comes to live the Mind-making life in accordance with the Bon of the Earth. In this way, ManWangManRae is the opportunity for human to get the evolutionary spontaneity continued from life to life.

YongByeonBuDongBon (用變不動本).
Usage changes but Bon does not move.

Both the role and usage change in the process of ManWangManRae. But in YongByeonBuDongBon (用變不動本), Bon does not change according to the usage. Bon symbolizes independence, and the purpose of the independent does not change. This is the meaning of MuJinBon (無盡本) which is always the same. Even if the usage changes, the being can keep the purpose for evolution, so the evolution continues. If a being has

BuDongBon (不動本) during an evolutionary process, only usage changes according to each life from then on. Byeon (變) of YongByeonBuDongBon (用變不動本) means that the change occurs in a state of having Bon as human. So it is not like Hwa (化) of HwaSam (化三) which means complete renewal. Through this process, necessary experience for evolution is accumulated and the stage of evolution becomes higher. Therefore, Bon of YongByeonBuDongBon basically means the Bon of the Earth. The Bon at this moment is Bon which makes One flow with the purpose of the finish.

BuDongBon means just Bon of human. It is different from an individual, the Self, having Bon. BuDongBon is a group circulation that being born and stopping occur within the existential character of human. Only the existential uncertainty as human has disappeared. It is the stage of Pal (Eight) in the IlMyoYeon where human has BuDongBon as human like this. Different from Chil (Seven), Pal (Eight) is able to move towards the finish being repeated as human. The Cheon Bu Gyeong shows the process through YongByeonBuDongBon where the evolutionary being, human becomes independent from all creation and then becomes self-reliant as human.

This is because the purpose of evolution is for the Bon of the Earth to make a being circulate from all creation to human and from human to the independent Self. YongByeonBuDongBon is the existential evolution for this that usage changes with the fixed existence.

The existential evolution of human is a process of having Bon like the Earth. For this, human gets an opportunity through ManWangManRae (萬往萬來), and has the evolutionary Bon fixed as the same existence through YongByeonBuDongBon (用變不動本). However, even though the existence of mankind has been gained, Bon as One being has not been achieved yet. BuDongBon also means that the original Bon does not change regardless of the usage of the current life. This is because the Earth gives different usage from the evolutionary stage for the imitation and confirmation for evolution. YongByeon (用變) is a process of diversification in order to have the Mind. A king, a peasant or an ascetic differs only in the picture of life. Therefore, the evolutionary stage of human can be known only when we can see the existential Bon rather than the usage or the role. In this way, having BuDongBon as human through YongByeonBuDongBon is the selection and concentration for evolution. Through this process, when human arrives at the state of complete BuDongBon where Bon never moves, that is the state where all things are connected as one, then he has BonSim (本心).

YongByeonBuDongBon is human going through the process of various lives. Because the Bon stipulating the existence does not change, the purpose and direction are maintained consistently. BuDongBon (不動本) originally means that Bon of all creation is the same regardless of character or shape. In the evolutionary stage of IlMyoYeon, it is used to indicate that Bon as human is maintained. Therefore during IlMyoYeon, different from the all creation or Chil (Seven) which are not determined to evolve into human, human who is Pal (Eight) goes through YongByeon in a state where Bon for the finish continues. The purpose of the Earth is constant and certain, so the evolutionary regression of a being does not occur. Therefore, the usage of IlMyoYeon is to eliminate many things that comprises human, and to create the state of BuDong (不動, not move) with a single Bon. And through this process, it is the Mind that is only left in human as Bon. YongByeonBuDongBon shows that the flow of human for this cannot escape from the stage of SaengChilPalGu (生七八九). The existence of human continues from when it was shared with all creation until it becomes independent as only human's and then becomes self-reliant as an individual, the Self, to arrive at the finish. This is the way of natural concentration through IlMyoYeon. It is selecting the evolutionary main agent going through ManWangManRae, YongByeonBuDongBon and BonSim (本心). In this way, BonSim (本心) symbolizes that the main agent of evolution changed from all creation to human, and then again to an individual, the Self.

Verse 8

BonSim (本心),

Bon is Sim (the Mind)

BonTaeYangAngMyeong (本太陽昂明),

When looking up to Bon, the brightness of the Sun

InJungCheonJiIl (人中天地一).

Cheon and Ji becomes Il (One) inside In (Human).

本 Bon : the Root / 心 Sim : the Mind /
本 Bon : the Root / 太陽 Taeyang : the sun / 昂 Ang : follow / 明 Myeong : the brightness
人 In : human / 中 Jung : in, center / 天 Cheon : the sky / 地 Ji : the Earth, earth / 一 Il : One

BonSim (本心),
Bon is Sim (the Mind)

Bon is the root that each of the cosmos, the Earth, and human has gained. All of them were sequentially gained from the single Mu. When human becomes a state of BuDongBon (不動本), then he can pursue the Bon of the Earth. And BonSim (本心) is containing the earthly Mu by combining CheonJiIn into one in the process of pursuing the Bon. BonSim (本心) is the state in which CheonJiIn that came from SamGeuk is combined into one. Only one among CheonJiIn remains at SamGeuk. In this state, Bon of the cosmos, the Earth, and human are connected and the cosmic evolution begins. Because BonSim is that Mu of the cosmos passes through Bon of the Earth and then settles down in human. Like this, the Cheon Bu Gyeong expresses the evolutionary stages by dividing the same thing into Mu of the cosmos, Bon of the Earth and the Mind of human. Therefore, the fact that human has gone through the earthly evolution and gained BonSim means that he has gained the qualification for the cosmic evolution. He becomes the state of repeating circulation as the Self. From this moment, the only thing required is the brightness of the sun which is needed to evolve into the Mu of the cosmos. Through this, human can reach the state of Mu of SeokSamGeuk (析三極) which is Bon of the Earth.

The goal of IlMyoYeon (一妙衍) is that Mu, the Mind of the cosmos passes through Bon, the Mind of the Earth and reaches the Mind of human and becomes Mu. In this way the Mu of the cosmos passes through the earthly evolutionary process and then becomes held as Bon of human. BonSim (本心) symbolizes Gu (Nine) in SaengChilPalGu (生七八九) which is the evolutionary stage of human. BonSim is required for the evolutionary goal of human, InJungCheonJiIl (人中天地一) of Sip (Ten). And BonSim is what contains CheonJi (天地) of CheonJiIn SamJae with BuDongBon (不動本). Thereby human gains the experience of containing CheonJi-like property of SamGeuk which made SamJae. It is the process of WonSiBanBon (原始返本) that is returning to the cosmic Mu by reunifying the earthly Mu that was divided into from SamGeuk to human. Bon is the symbol of independent One that the cosmos, the Earth and human have in common. By having BonSim, human becomes placed in the process of the cosmic evolution. From that moment, like the Earth moves around the sun, human also moves around the sun as the Self, an individual being. At last human lives as a being of the self. In order to live as the Self, human has struggled to live a life where the Mind settles as Bon from old times.

The cosmic Mu is the root of everything that exists. This is the reason why the Cheon Bu Gyeong starts with IlSiMuSill (一始無始一) which brings forth the fact that the Earth has begun from Mu, and its Bon is Mu. Therefore, if human has Bon as an independent being, then the Bon is also in a state of Mu. The name of the earthly Bon is SamGeuk, and that of the human Bon is the Mind. Like this, InJung (人中) is a state in which human is Mu with BonSim, and human becomes one Geuk among SamGeuk (three Geuks). The Mu of this moment is not the cosmic Mu of MuSill that SamGeuk is created from, but the earthly Mu which is created from SamGeuk. And it is InJungCheonJiIl (人中天地一) that is gained in this state through the brightness of the sun which is the cosmic Bon. BonSim is what connects human with the cosmos through Bon, and it can be known by human doing TaeYangAngMyeong (太陽昻明) like the Earth. Therefore, human can be the same state of the Earth through containing CheonJi-like property of SamGeuk in the Mind.

It is only the Mind that does not change in human. A state of ManWangManRae (萬往萬來) is instinct, and what human has in a state of BuDongBon (不動本) is not the Mind, but emotion. Human regards the emotion as the Mind, so he cannot have the Mind. If human has the Mind, he naturally and constantly continues like BuDongBon of the Earth. It is like the Earth follows the brightness of the sun. When a being of Yuk (Six) with a place for the Mind has gone through the process of Chil (Seven) and Pal (Eight) and arrives at Gu (Nine) that has Bon, then the being has the Mind. BonSim shows that instinct and emotion in a state of Yuk (Six), Chil (Seven) and Pal (Eight) are different from the Mind. Building a house of the Mind in a place for the Mind is the responsibility of human as well as the path of evolution. The path is not outside but inside human, and there is no way to create the Mind outside human. Like the same principle as the Earth creates human inside it with the brightness of the sun, the Mind is created inside human. Only after the Mind is created, human can pursue what is outside like the Earth. This is the difference between pursuing the Bon of the Earth which is SamGeuk to create the Mind through CheonJiIn, and pursuing the sun which is the Bon of the cosmos to become InJungCheonJiIl through SamGeuk. This is the reason why the Cheon Bu Gyeong shows the evolutionary way of Mu with independence and self-reliance.

Human can have the unchanging Mind only when he contains BuDongBon (不動本) of CheonJi among CheonJiIn. If human resembles the brightness of the sun, the Mind of the cosmos, then he can contain CheonJi-like property of SamGeuk as Mu. Existential BanBonHwanWon (返本還原) through the Mind of human is the role of human in accordance with the purpose of the cosmos. If human becomes the being with the earthly Mu by finishing the existential evolution, then he can begin to evolve into the cosmic Mu. This is because Mu, the Mind, settles inside human. When the Mind becomes Bon of human, then he comes to pursue the brightness of the sun by himself like the Earth. The earth got the nature when it had the independent Mu through IlSiMuSiIl (一始無始一). The brightness of the sun is the Bon of life for the Earth, and it helps human exceed his existential limit. The cosmos can refine only the human who has reached BonSim by itself. The reason why human has BonSim is to receive the help, and it is the prerequisite condition to become a state of Sip (Ten) through the brightness of the sun. Human can start this process only after he overcome the conceptual limit by himself that human is the earthly being. This is possible when human realizes that everybody has the opportunity to become God.

BonTaeYangAngMyeong (本太陽昂明),
When looking up to Bon, the brightness of the Sun

The bon of the earthly evolution is the sun. It is thanks to the existence of the sun that the Earth can keep alive and evolve all creation. Human can cross his border by directly having the sun as Bon, which is the meaning of BonTaeYangAngMyeong (本太陽昂明). From the moment of having BonSim, human escapes from the earthly causality and then pursues the brightness of the sun. When human has BonSim through pursuing the earthly Bon, then the switch to TaeYangAngMyeong (太陽昂明) happens naturally. This is because the evolutionary life of human is taking after the Earth. Therefore, after the earthly evolution is finished through BonSim, the cosmic evolution of BonTaeYangAngMyeong begins. The reason that the Cheon Bu Gyeong placed BonTaeYang (本太陽) next to BonSim is to show that human and the cosmos come to be connected regardless of the Earth. It shows the way how human becomes the same state as the Earth by pursuing the sun, not the Earth. Looking up to the sun without the Mind is only sharing the brightness that the Earth holds.

The sun is One which has begun for the purpose of the cosmos. Not like the Earth that has an influence on the beings inside it, the sun influences the beings outside it. The difference between the Earth and the sun is the same as that between human and God. Therefore, from the perspective of the cosmos, the sun symbolizes the more evolved being than the Earth. The sun is a completed form of evolution in accordance with the purpose of the cosmos. With the earthly principle human cannot escape from the earthly Mu. For this reason, human needs to switch the subject of pursuit from SamGeuk, Bon of the Earth, to the sun, Bon of the cosmos. The evolutionary role of the Earth ends when human arrives at BonSim where he can look up to the brightness of the sun. The cosmos has tied the sun to the Earth, and human evolves with the indirect brightness of the sun through the Earth.

It is thanks to the sun that human can evolve inside the Earth. BonTaeYang (本太陽) shows that the cosmos makes human not lose his way to reborn as a being of the cosmos. Because the purpose of the cosmos is to evolve human from the earthly Mu based being into the cosmic Mu based being. The flow of the cosmos is not so meaningless as it creates human for the Earth. The cosmos shows this through the sun. The Earth cannot survive without the sun, and all lives in the Earth also cannot live without it. This existential absoluteness of the sun suggests the direction of evolution for both the Earth and the earthly beings. This is because the Earth has been created under the design that its survival and flow are only possible through the sun. For this reason, when human arrives at BonSim, he naturally changes to the being that relies on the sun. The brightness (明) symbolizes the sun like this.

Human should pursue the sun indirectly before he has the Mind as Bon. This is because it is not possible for him to pursue the brightness of the sun as it is. The teachings and scriptures left by the humans who became Gods are about the brightness of the sun and to help human make the Mind through pursuing them. For this reason, scriptures such as the Cheon Bu Gyeong, the Do Deok Gyeong (道德經, Tao Te Ching in Chinese), and the Yeok Gyeong (易經, I Ching in Chinese) do not cover relativity. They just mention about the existence through Bon. From the moment that human has the Mind, nothing is needed except the brightness of the sun. The sun is the only cosmic being that human can feel directly. This is the reason why the Earth is designed to have the sun as source of life. The sun is God of the cosmos and AngMyeong (昂明) is the divinity (神性) that teaches human the way how to be equal to the Earth. Like the Earth raises all creation through the brightness and strength of the sun, human can be a being equal to the Earth through receiving the brightness of the sun directly.

The only thing needed for the finish of human is the brightness of the sun. No other things are required in the evolutionary process of the Earth and human. But, because human does not know the way how to pursue the sun directly, so human goes through the evolutionary process up to Gu (Nine). Buddha, Jesus, and Lao Tzu clearly teach that human cannot pursue the sun without the Mind. The cosmos that creates the One of the Earth and numerous Ones inside the earth is symbolized as the sun. And it is the brightness of the sun that makes flowers bloom in human BonSim that those beings gained through the evolutionary process. For this, the Earth and all creation are designed to have the sun as their source, and this cosmic design makes it possible for human to evolve in sharing Bon of the cosmos with the Earth. That is why the Cheon Bu Gyeong explains the process where human has the Mind as Bon at great length, but shows only the standard and existential form about the finish process with BonTaeYangAngMyeong (本太陽昂明) and InJungCheonJiIl (人中天地一). This is why Gods and Saints have taught that human cannot find the answers outside the Mind. If human can look up to the brightness of the sun, then he can be the Mu of the complete One at any time. The reason why human can contain the Earth with the Mind is that he is based on the Mu of the cosmos.

InJungCheonJill (人中天地一).
Cheon and Ji becomes Il (One) inside In (Human).

The Earth is a state of One where SamGeuk contains human with CheonJiIn SamJae. On the other hand, InJungCheonJiIl (人中天地一) is that human contains the CheonJi of SamGeuk with the Mind and becomes One. It is for human to become independent from the Earth and then self-reliant, and the state is Mu where being, time and space are one. It symbolizes human who continues as the cosmic being like the Earth. What was separated into SamGeuk and SamJae for the earthly evolution is combined into one inside human. Through InJungCheonJiIl human becomes able to exist in the cosmos with Sip (Ten), the cosmic Mu, as his Bon like the Earth. Therefore, human evolution inside the Earth is not a new path. It is going through BanBonHwanWon to return to the original form which is the state of MuSill before the separation of the Earth. The brightness of the sun came inside the Mind through the process of creating the Mind with the brightness. Like the brightness of the sun connects the Earth and the cosmos, human crosses the border between the Earth and the cosmos by pursuing the brightness with the Mind. Arriving at this state is InJungCheonJiIl, and through this the cosmic evolution in the Earth is finished.

The earthly evolution cannot be done by pioneering unknown path. It is the same way as a child becomes a parent by following its parents, and it is accomplished by following the process where the Earth has changed. For this reason, the evolutionary process of human is tracing back the change process of the Earth, from the being of human to SamJae and again from SamJae to SamGeuk. Through this process, human makes the Mind with the Mu of the Earth as Bon, and arrives at IlJongMuJongIl (一終無終一) with the Mu of the cosmos as Bon. The brightness of the sun is the door that transports human from the Earth to the cosmos, and InJungCheonJiIl (人中天地一) is the qualification to pass through the door. The evolution of the Earth is to place human at the time of MuSiIl when the Earth began as One. Therefore, InJungCheonJiIl is also achieved by the principle of UnSamSaSeong which is the characteristic of the earthly evolution. This is the reason why human, the being with the cosmic divinity is awakened through the sun in the Earth separated from the cosmic Mu.

The Earth is a greenhouse of the cosmos that bears human with its own time and space, and human evolves in the greenhouse to go out into the cosmos by himself. The value of human is in that all creation and CheonJi made human together in one accord to let him go outside the greenhouse. Therefore, it is only human that can reach the Mu as the original Sip (Ten). Gu (Nine) is that human contains 'Sam (Three) held by the sky', 'Sam (Three) held by Earth', and 'Sam (Three) held by all creation' in 2 Un through the process of 3 Un. The Sip (Ten) where human has arrived through this process is the Mu with new character having the same size as the Earth. While the Earth is a being for the things inside it, human who arrived at Sip (Ten) exchanges influences with the things outside him like the sun. For this reason, Buddha, Jesus and Lao Tzu who have arrived at InJungCheonJiIl become Gods who influence the beings outside them like the sun. The Earth has become the being for the finish of human as a result of evolution. However, this is possible only when human has BonSim. The Mind of human is Mu, and human and the cosmos can become one when human is Mu. Human can connects the cosmic property between human and the cosmos by the Mu, so he can be MuJongIl.

The Earth made for the purpose and human who has evolved by himself are different in the existential characteristics and roles. Therefore, human who can do the same role as the Earth is separated and called God. Like this, when the existential size becomes the same as what has begun as One but the existence becomes different, it is said that what has begun finished. The place from which One begins is Mu, the state in which One begins is also Mu, and the state in which One finishes is Mu as well. On the Earth, only human has the Mind that can make it possible, which is InNaeCheon. As CheonJiIn SamJae made in the space of SamGeuk become one, human comes to have the Mind as Bon. As human becomes the same as one Geuk of SamGeuk (three Geuks) where SamJae had been placed, he becomes InJung which is one Geuk. InJung of InJungCheonJiIl is the Mu of empty space before SamJae has been created in SamGeuk, and CheonJi are two Geuks of SamGeuk, and Il (One) symbolizes human as the being holding the SamGeuk in the same state as the Earth. Like this, BonSim is that SamJae has become one, and InJungCheonJiIl is that SamGeuk has become one. IlMyoYeon is finished with that human becomes InJungCheonJiIl which is the same state as the Bon of the Earth through the principle of SamGeuk creating BonSim with SamJae.

Verse 9

IlJongMuJongIl (一終無終一).

Il (One) finishes and it finishes as Mu

一 Il : One / 終 Jong : finish / 無 Mu : the state before the Big Bang, zero, nothing, extinct / 終 Jong : finish / 一 Il : One

IlJongMuJongIl (一終無終一).

Il (One) finishes and it finishes as Mu.

Mu of IlJongMuJongIl (一終無終一) is not that what has begun 'disappeared', but that it has become a state of Mu. The Mu at this moment is not only the finish of One but also the Mu as a being which makes a new beginning. Like this, MuJongIl is that human holds the MuSill state of the Earth through IlJong. A being created in the time and space of MuSill becomes the being that holds the time and space through MuJongIl. It is the cosmic being, God. IlJong (一終) is that the change and the evolution started from MuSill has finished, not that what has begun as One finished. It means that through the earthly evolution human goes through IlJong and becomes MuJongIl, but the Earth continues to flow as it does. This is because the Earth is not for a single human. MuJongIl is the finish in a state of Mu, which means that a new One which is different from what has begun as One is created in the cosmos. The number of 'this new One of Mu' is Sip (Ten) which is the same number as the Earth. Sip (10) means that Il (1) becomes Mu (0).

In the time and space of Sip (Ten), the maximum of

possible evolution is Sip (Ten). Human who arrived at Sip (Ten) becomes different from the Earth which can exist only as time and space. He becomes a free being that is being, time and space at once. Like this, because human is being, time and space at the same time, he is different from the star whose existence is only time and space in the cosmos. The evolution in the Earth is that time and space creates a being and put the time and space into the being. On the other hand, the evolution in the cosmos is only possible for those subjects that are beings, time and space at once. This is the reason that the star itself cannot evolve in the cosmos. It is God that is able to evolve in the cosmos, and from that moment he can walk the evolutionary path in the cosmos as God rather than the earthly evolution. This is the principle of the cosmic evolutionary path walked by God. MuJongIl (無終一) is not that a new being is created, but the being that has gone through InJungCheonJiIl continues as Mu. The reason why a bigger state of Mu than Gu (Nine) is called Sip (Ten) is that the Mu where One has reached by the finish becomes a new starting point by itself. Like Sip (Ten) in the cosmos symbolizes the Earth as the cosmic being, the Sip (Ten) of MuJongIl symbolizes human as the cosmic being. Both MuSiIl and MuJongIl are the states that hold the beginning.

Mu is applied to the beginning of the cosmos, the Earth and all creation on the same principle. The Cheon Bu Gyeong expresses by IlJongMuJongIl (一終無終一) that a being that was born through IlSiMuSill (一始無始一) evolves from the earthly life into the cosmic life. This means that human is completely free from the earthly time and space and the material limits. This is the reason why the absolute Mu creates the cosmos and the Earth to give birth to human. For this reason, the Cheon Bu Gyeong can be the scripture in accordance with the purpose of the cosmos, in other words the scripture that holds the principle of the cosmic evolution. The Cheon Bu Gyeong explains that the reason that the Earth exists in the cosmos is the evolutionary purpose of the cosmos. Stars such as the Earth which have evolved as the time and space in the cosmos were made to be the source of supply that evolve beings like human and supply them to the cosmos. This can be known that after they have achieved the purpose by making a being arrive at IlJong in the cosmos, they continue for another IlJong.

Through IlJongMuJongIl (一終無終一), the Earth gives

birth to a God into the cosmos from human in its womb. This is the result in accordance with the purpose of the absolute Mu creating the cosmos and the Earth. Human born in the cosmos will walk the path of maturity in a state of MuJongIl and arrive at the absolute Mu. Human gone through IlJong can perform the same role of the Earth. This is because he is a newly created being after achieving the purpose through MuJongIl (無終一). Therefore in the Cheon Bu Gyeong, IlSiMuSiIl (一始無始一) is about the time and space called the Earth and IlJongMuJongIl (一終無終一) is about that the being within the time and space corresponds to the purpose of the sky. It is only in case of human who is being, time and space at once, that is God that IlSiMuSiIl (一始無始一) and IlJongMuJongIl (一終無終一) function as one. Human who had walked the path passed down the Cheon Bu Gyeong to teach that this is possible for every human. Like this, human can begin again in a new area as the same being. Or he can become God like the Gods of the existing religions. This can be understood by having the cosmic time and concepts rather than the earthly time and concepts.

The Cheon Bu Gyeong captures the evolutionary process of Mu from the human perspective. The purpose is to create a being equal to the cosmos that is being, time and space at once. IlJongMuJongIl (一終無終一) is that human born as such being begins to evolve into being, time and space that is equal to the cosmos in size. The cosmos made the Earth begin for this purpose. This shows clearly that human is the being that doesn't have to be greedy for anything but the Mind. It also states the reason why human with the complete Mind doesn't have interest in anything but the brightness. Human must realize that what exist and the changes are in fact Mu. The original Mu exists as both the visible and the invisible, so it does not have any relative concept. Human separates it into what exists and does not, and understands the complexity of the cosmos separately. Therefore, it is when human breaks away from the relative concept of Mu that he can understand BuDongBon, and it is when human is free from the thing shown and the usage of life that they can create the Mind. Through this human can clearly know why the Earth begins as One and makes human finish as One. By following the path, human can be the human of MuJongIl that is free from existence, time and space, and can continue to exist.

The Cheon Bu Gyeong says that when human arrives at MuJongIl through IlJong the life of the Self goes over to the cosmic level from the earthly level. This is the path walked by Buddha, as well as by Jesus and Lao Tzu. The Cheon Bu Gyeong proves this path with only eighty-one letters, and thereby shows that this is clearly the truth. Through this, it tries to teach that the purpose of human is to walk the path of God. The Cheon Bu Gyeong recommends that human live a life not as metempsychosis of the earthly human but continuing as the cosmic human. The Cheon Bu Gyeong shows the path of God, and the Yeok Gyeong (易經, I Ching in Chinese) and the Do Deok Gyeong (道德經, Tao Te Ching in Chinese) are the Mind which builds a bridge on the path. IlJongMuJongIl (一終無終一) is the starting point for a new beginning in accordance with the purpose of the cosmos. If human arrives at MuJongIl, then he can help other humans finish on the Earth in the form of God. Or he can restart the path to be the God of the cosmos by choosing the path to begin as a cosmic being. It is walking as God after having walked the path of becoming God. It is the image of Mu shown by IlJongMuJongIl (一終無終一) which is connected by the finish and continuation.

In the cosmos, the sun is God to the Earth and the Earth is God to all creation. And it is human that these two Gods made with evolutionary pain. Here comes the distinction of InNaeCheon (人乃天) of human. Thanks to the two Gods which are the cosmos and the Earth, human can become God by himself through the finish. That is why the absolute Mu created the cosmos and the Earth. The sun holds the divinity of these two beings. This way is not different from that parents give birth to children and those children become parents, then again give birth to children. It just seems different depending on whether it happens "among humans" or "in the universe or the Earth". The Cheon Bu Gyeong is left behind by the people from the sky. Hwan Woong and the 3000 people from the sky are the symbol of people who walk the path of evolution in the cosmos through IlJongMuJongIl (一終無終一). And the fact that they came down from the sky is to inform human that it is not so hard to do. The image of life for this is HongIkInGhan (弘益人間) which means 'benefit human far and wide', and those who live this life are HongIkInGhan which means 'people who benefits human far and wide'. Therefore, HongIkInGhan is a human who has BonSim or in a state of InJungCheonJiIl, and the world where they live is

IHwaSeGye (理化世界, The world of Ihwa). This is why the people from the sky left behind the Cheon Bu Gyeong, to show the principle of the cosmic brightness through their lifestyle, HongIkInGhan and IHwaSeGye. The Cheon Bu Gyeong is the story of the Earth and human living in the cosmos which is told using IlSiMuSiIl (一始無始一) and IlJongMuJongIl (一終無終一). If human is connected with the beginning of IlSiMuSiIl (一始無始一) in the cosmos after IlJongMuJongIl (一終無終一) then the new story of the cosmos and human will start from the Self. It is that human has become the sky.

The principle of a cosmic evolutionary path walked by God

Cheon Bu Gyeong 天符經

Copyright © 2014 Sang-Young Han

Edited by Ho-Young Lee, Sang-A Park
Translated by Seong-Uk Park / Kwang-Soo Shin

Published in the Republic of korea by Publishing Jisikgonggam,
112, Gyeondalsan-ro 225beon-gil, Ilsandong-gu, Goyang-si,
Gyeonggi-do, Korea.

Web: www.bookdaum.com
Email: bookon@daum.net
Tel: +82 2 3141 2700

Paperback ISBN: 979-11-5622-046-6 (13150)
CIP 2014029747
First published in paperback October 2014.

All rights reserved.
No part of this publication may be reproduced, stored in a retrieval
system or transmitted in any form or by any means, where electronic,
mechanical, photocopying, recording of otherwise, without the
written permission of the author.

This book is sold subject to the condition that it shall not, by way of
trade or otherwise, be lent, resold, hired out or otherwise circulated
without the publisher's prior consent in any form of binding or
cover other than that in which it is published and without a similar
condition including this condition being imposed on the subsequent
purchaser.